THEOLOGIA CRUCIS

CASCADE COMPANIONS

The Christian theological tradition provides an embarrassment of riches: from Scripture to modern scholarship, we are blessed with a vast and complex theological inheritance. And yet this feast of traditional riches is too frequently inaccessible to the general reader.

The Cascade Companions series addresses the challenge by publishing books that combine academic rigor with broad appeal and readability. They aim to introduce nonspecialist readers to that vital storehouse of authors, documents, themes, histories, arguments, and movements that comprise this heritage with brief yet compelling volumes.

TITLES IN THIS SERIES:

Reading Augustine by Jason Byassee
Conflict, Community, and Honor by John H. Elliott
An Introduction to the Desert Fathers by Jason Byassee
Reading Paul by Michael J. Gorman
Theology and Culture by D. Stephen Long
Creation and Evolution by Tatha Wiley
Theological Interpretation of Scripture by Stephen Fowl
Reading Bonhoeffer by Geffrey B. Kelly
Justpeace Ethics by Jarem Sawatsky
Feminism and Christianity by Caryn D. Griswold
Angels, Worms, and Bogeys by Michelle A. Clifton-Soderstrom
Christianity and Politics by C. C. Pecknold
A Way to Scholasticism by Peter S. Dillard
Theological Theodicy by Daniel Castelo
The Letter to the Hebrews in Social-Scientific Perspective by David A. deSilva
Basil of Caesarea by Andrew Radde-Galwitz
A Guide to St. Symeon the New Theologian by Hannah Hunt
Reading John by Christopher W. Skinner
Forgiveness by Anthony Bash
Jacob Arminius by Rustin Brian
Reading Jeremiah by Jack Lundbom
John Calvin by Donald McKim

THEOLOGIA CRUCIS

A Companion to the Theology of the Cross

ROBERT CADY SALER

CASCADE *Books* • Eugene, Oregon

THEOLOGIA CRUCIS
A Companion to the Theology of the Cross

Cascade Companions

Cascade Books
An Imprint of Wipf and Stock Publishers
199 W. 8th Ave., Suite 3
Eugene, OR 97401

www.wipfandstock.com

PAPERBACK ISBN: 978-1-4982-3191-6
HARDCOVER ISBN: 978-1-4982-3193-0
EBOOK ISBN: 978-1-4982-3192-3

Cataloguing-in-Publication data:

Names: Robert Cady Saler.

Title: Theologia crucis : a companion to the theology of the cross / Robert Cady Saler.

Description: Eugene, OR: Pickwick Publications, 2016 | Series: if applicable | Includes bibliographical references and index.

Identifiers: ISBN 978-1-4982-3191-6 (paperback) | ISBN 978-1-4982-3193-0 (hardcover) | ISBN 978-1-4982-3192-3 (ebook)

Subjects: LCSH: Jesus Christ—Crucifixion | Atonement | Theology of the cross |

Classification: BT453 S2 2016 (paperback) | BT453 (ebook)

Manufactured in the U.S.A. 09/27/16

CONTENTS

INTRODUCTION

For Christ did not send me to baptize but to proclaim the gospel, and not with eloquent wisdom, so that the cross of Christ might not be emptied of its power. For the message about the cross is foolishness to those who are perishing, but to us who are being saved it is the power of God. For it is written, "I will destroy the wisdom of the wise, and the discernment of the discerning I will thwart."

Where is the one who is wise? Where is the scribe? Where is the debater of this age? Has not God made foolish the wisdom of the world? For since, in the wisdom of God, the world did not know God through wisdom, God decided, through the foolishness of our proclamation, to save those who believe. For Jews demand signs and Greeks desire wisdom, but we proclaim Christ crucified, a stumbling-block to Jews and foolishness to Gentiles, but to those who are the called, both Jews and Greeks, Christ the power of God and the wisdom of God. For God's foolishness is wiser than human wisdom, and God's weakness is stronger than human strength. Consider your own call, brothers and sisters: not many of you were wise by human standards, not many were powerful, not many were of noble birth. But God chose what is foolish in the world to shame the wise; God chose what is weak in the world to shame the strong; God chose what is low and despised in the world, things that are not, to reduce to nothing things that are, so that no one might boast in the presence of God. He is the source of your life in Christ Jesus, who became for us wisdom from God, and righteousness and sanctification and redemption, in order that, as it is written, "Let the one who boasts, boast in*the Lord."

—1 Cor 1:17–31[1]

Paul could not conceive of an uncrucified savior.

Moreover, in building that savior's church, the Christian movement, he apparently had no conception of a community without the scandal of the cross at the center of its life.[2] Indeed, in his letter to the Corinthians, Paul would appeal to the fact that, in contrast to those who came to the churches with impressive appearance and speech, he is more akin to the crucified Jesus in that he presents weakness in order to let God's strength shine through:

> For I decided to know nothing among you except Jesus Christ, and him crucified. And I came to you in weakness and in fear and in much trembling. My speech and my proclamation were not with plausible words of wisdom, but with a demonstration of the Spirit and of power, so that

1. All biblical quotations taken from the New Revised Standard Version (NRSV) unless otherwise noted.

2. The same can be said about the gospel narratives; indeed, the New Testament scholar Martin Kähler once famously remarked that "The gospels are the history of the passion with a long introduction." Cf. Kähler, *So-Called Historical Jesus*, 80.

> your faith might rest not on human wisdom but on the power of God. (1 Cor 2:2–5)

Similarly, he asks the church to consider that most of the members of these churches were from similarly low background; like Paul, their weakness mirrors the weakness of the broken Christ on the cross precisely so that they could reflect the peculiar wisdom of God rather than human standards, since "God chose what is foolish in the world to shame the wise; God chose what is weak in the world to shame the strong; God chose what is low and despised in the world, things that are not, to reduce to nothing things that are, so that no one might boast in the presence of God" (1 Cor 1:27–28).

Paul, the apostle of the crucified, sees the essence of the church as a community that models to the world the same method of salvation that God uses: human weakness revealing the true nature of divine power. This theology of the cross that gives rise to the community of the cross has both a preaching function (proclaiming the gospel) but also what we might call a deconstructive function; that is, part of the message of the gospel is that the world's way of accounting that which is valuable and that which is to be despised is in the process of being turned upside down. This process is inaugurated in the cross and resurrection of Christ and continues in our time wherever the call to the cross is heeded.

A few centuries later, as the movement gained momentum and debates over the nature of Christ intensified, nascent Christian orthodoxy rejected multiple options that depicted Christ as less than fully divine, and an equal number that construed him as less than fully human. In what became enshrined in the creeds of the church, only a fully divine and fully human savior could suffice for salvation. While there were a number of reasons why Christian orthodoxy came to be identified with the belief that Christ is simultaneously fully divine and fully human, a large subtext of the debate was the cross. If Christ was less than fully divine, then it is not God on the cross. If Christ is less than fully human, then God is not really suffering on the cross. If he is both, then the implication is clear: Christian God-talk cannot dispense with the scandalous notion that it is truly God on the cross.[3]

What difference does it make that the one Christians venerate as the Messiah was crucified? What difference does it make to theology—the Christian movement's ongoing thinking about the nature of God and the world—that the cross of a broken man who *also* participates uniquely in the divine life stands as its central symbol? How do Christians theologize about the cross?

If one were to view the cross within the confines of Christian discourse alone, then one would likely receive the impression that the crucifixion of Jesus of Nazareth—known to his followers since as Jesus the Christ—was an event of singular importance, if not the central event of human history.

This is the case not only because of the fact that Christian theology has ascribed uniquely salvific power to the event, but also because church hymnody, preaching, and art has long given the impression that Jesus' sufferings on the cross were of a uniquely terrible nature. From hymns such as Johann Heerman's "Ah, Holy Jesus" to Mel Gibson's 2004 film *The Passion of the Christ*, lavish attention has been paid to the details of the pain (*passio*) suffered by Jesus as those details are recounted in the gospel narratives and embellished in the Christian narrative imagination. Indeed, from the patristic period onward (although not reaching its deepest flourishes until the medieval period), the link between

3. Cf. Vítor Westhelle, *Scandalous God.*

the intensity of Jesus' suffering and the salvific character of those sufferings—a link in fact proposing direct proportionality (the more intense the suffering, the more salvific the event)—has been a key part of the operative Christian logic of salvation. In his influential fourth-century text *On the Incarnation of the Word*, Athanasius, the great champion of nascent orthodox Christology, counseled that "if any of our own people [Christians] also inquire, not from love of debate but from love of learning, why he suffered death in no other way save on the cross, let him also be told that no other way than this was good for us, and that it was well that the Lord suffered this for our sakes."[4]

Later medieval writings such as the poem *Salvi mundi salutare* (meditating on the various wounded parts of Christ's crucified body) and the copious "blood" imagery present in such mystical writers as Catherine of Siena would carry this focus on the intensity of Christ's suffering forward, providing a rich vocabulary for later Christian traditions to appropriate in theology, worship, and veneration of the cross in such a way that the suffering, death, and resurrection of Jesus become, in the words of Alan Lewis, "a Word that could confound our intellects, overturn our morality, and shock, surprise, and change us body, mind, and spirit."[5]

However, when one situates the crucifixion within the broader context of imperial Roman politics, then one is confronted with another twist in the tale: executions such as the one suffered by Jesus were relatively commonplace in the Roman empire. While those who shared Jesus' religion would have inevitably overlain the events of his cross with the curse imparted by their scriptures (Deut 21:23), within the hegemony imparted by Roman imperialism (as well as

4. Athanasius, "On the Incarnation," 79.

5. Lewis, *Between Cross and Resurrection*, 17.

that of other imperial contenders of the day) the symbol of the cross would have been all the more terrifying for its ubiquity; it is inevitable, so the narrative goes, that insurrection against the pretense of imperial peace will end in horrifying violence for rebels.

These two historical facts—that crucifixion was a (horrifically) banal event in the *pax Romanum* even as it has been claimed as foundational for the Christian faith—are emblematic of the relationship that the cross has had to Christian theology for the past two millennia. A central claim of Christianity is that the God of Jesus Christ is manifest to the world, not primarily in the form of theophany and power, but in the form of weakness and suffering; thus, in order to "find God" and God's actions in the world, it is precisely in the everyday suffering of humanity and creation—even the most terrible suffering—that one should look. Indeed, it is precisely because suffering is so ubiquitous (including suffering at the hands of injustice, the "passions" of those who are victims of theological and political lust for domination no less than was Christ himself) that the centrality of the cross to faith remains so compelling to many.

Theologia crucis, the "theology of the cross," is the theological strand within the Christian tradition that emphasizes this truth and endeavors to make it central for Christian theological thinking. Theology of the cross invokes the cross in order to try to speak rightly about the pain of the world and the God who, in Christ, involves the divine life in that pain—even unto death.

Theological reflection about the cross and its implications for theology has produced a vast swath of writings, and no one book can hope to summarize them all; indeed, summary is not at all my intention. Instead, this book provides some orientation strategies that will, in the best case scenario, inspire (and perhaps provisionally guide) further inquiry into the complex questions raised by the cross itself as well as its variegated career throughout the Christian theological imagination. We will examine some key currents of the theology of the cross, with no pretense towards being comprehensive. Rather, the hope is that the examples considered will be sufficiently emblematic of larger trends within the voluminous literature—literature that readers will then hopefully feel empowered to take on themselves.

Likewise, this book is not a history of the Christian use of the cross as a symbol, nor even an account of the many and various ways in which the cross has been theologized throughout the two-thousand-year history of the Christian tradition(s). As I will argue in the coming chapters, "theology of the cross" as it is commonly employed within contemporary theology has some very specific roots in the Reformation and the subsequent transition from the medieval period to modernity (in the West), and also the contemporary collapse of historical optimism on multiple fronts (including theology). My goal is to provide some overview and analysis of contemporary theological trends that begin with Luther's recovery of the *theologia crucis* in the Reformation period and continue in contemporary theology. Think of it as a "field guide" to the theology of the cross in our time.

Indeed, one of the key things that I hope readers take from the book is the sense that, while there is a great degree of variance in the deployment of the cross, *theologia crucis* has emerged within theology as a peculiar mode of theological inquiry that has as its main feature the following contention: the nature of Christ's death on the cross, and the entry of God in Godself into the human condition, has deep implications for how we view God and how we view the task of applying theology to ethics. The cross changes everything. *Theologia crucis* is critical theology.

SPEAKING AND STUTTERING

Every tour guide has opinions, and those paying to take the tour have a right to know them.

With that in mind, this book will proceed on the basis of two key theses.

First, and somewhat paradoxically, I would argue that what we will discover in the coming chapters is that, both historically and today, the cross operates as both a check upon theology (a hindrance to theology that causes self-confident theological discourse to "stammer") and as the condition that makes God-talk possible by undercutting the inevitability of projecting our standards onto God.

The danger of projection—articulated by the great Western "masters of suspicion" such as Karl Marx, Friedrich Nietzsche, and Sigmund Freud, and also their contemporary Ludwig Feuerbach—is one that haunts any talk about theological realities (God, salvation, providence, etc.).[6] For instance, slaveholders in the antebellum South understood God as both instituting and blessing the horrors of chattel slavery, a claim which we would now rightly understand to be self-interested, wishful, and deluded thinking on the part of the slaveowners and the preachers who encouraged their exploitation from the pulpit. But even in cases where projection is less malicious—e.g., the sincerely held belief that God personally reaches down and allows NFL quarterbacks to make game-winning touchdowns in the last seconds of the fourth quarter—its virtual inevitability threatens to shipwreck the entire enterprise of "God-talk."

6. Cf. Westphal, *Suspicion and Faith.*

If the trap of projection is so easy to fall into, then perhaps theology itself is too speculative to be viable.

However, to the extent that *theologia crucis* is the discipline of finding God's truth and God's actions in the least likely places—the battered body of a crucified criminal, the ugly and marginalized places of our own worlds—then this theology can make an imperfect but vital contribution keeping our projections of our own agendas onto God in check. Through sheer counterintuitiveness, the theology of the cross can give us an optics upon both our world and upon God that is produces enough veracity through discordance.

Second, like any interesting theological concept, the theology of the cross has lent itself to abuse and the support of oppression; however, the same symbol has also been taken up and utilized as a tool against oppressive concepts of God. In other words, depending on how the theology of the cross is understood and deployed, it can either be deadly or life-giving.

As much anecdotal evidence shows, the cross has given aid and comfort to those who seek to use theology to encourage victims in their sufferings in a manner that disempowers protest. Be it the wife who is told to "bear the cross" of abuse at the hands of her husband or the armies slaughtered at the hands of knights wielding cross-imprinted shields, the trail of bloodshed left by the abuse of the cross is damning and an indictment of the entire movement that bears Christ's name.

However, the same cross has, at various points in history and in a multitude of places today, also been a powerful means by which theologians and activists have theorized "the fundamental conflict between a mission directed towards life and the actually existing arrangements of the world, both religious and political."[7] The cross, the symbol of death, has been theologically appropriated and transformed into a symbol of rebellion of life against death. Indeed, when it comes to complex symbols, the greater the potency, the more potential to harm—and to bless. Put differently: the cross can become an idol precisely because of its centrality and power within the Christian tradition (not to mention the emotional intensity it tends to evoke!). But that same power can subvert ideology and idolatry—at least, such is the gamble that *theologia crucis* wages.

To take the two theses together, then: if the cross causes theological "stammer" by interrupting overconfident and projective speech about God, it also evokes speech by providing the basis by which Christians and others can understand how God chooses to interact with the ugliness of our world, and to do so salvifically. The cross is what allows theology to talk. But it is also what forces theology to stammer. And both of those are good things. Stammering keeps truthful talk from becoming boastful ideology. But both fidelity to God and life in the world force us to speak, and sometimes the only speech that can touch both realities at once is "staurocentric" ("cross-centered") theology. This will hopefully become more apparent in the chapters to come.

HOW THE DISCUSSION WILL PROCEED

One method for a book like this would be to simply go in order: to start with the Bible, to move then through the medieval period, on to Martin Luther, and then through to the modern period, surveying and cataloguing different cross-centered authors and theologies along the way. But this will not be our plan. This is because, even as theological

7. Jennings, *Transforming Atonement*, 224.

epochs have come and gone, theologizing about the cross has been more like an extended conversation than any sort of linear pattern of development. All theologians, of course, theologize in response to the circumstances on the ground in their day and age; however, almost never do theologians invent new themes whole cloth.

In the case of theology of the cross specifically, we will see that many of the most exciting contextual and global developments of this theology build upon what was already nascent in Luther's formulations. That said, I want to be clear that, even though I write as a Lutheran theologian, I do not mean for this statement to reflect some kind of Lutheran triumphalism. Indeed, Lutherans should be the first to admit not only that Luther himself (and the tradition that bears his name) often failed to live up to the radical theological potential of Luther's own *theologia crucis*, but that this potential has often borne fruit in contexts very different from what Luther envisioned. Luther applied the critical potential of the cross to the abuses of power of the medieval church; however, he stopped short (disastrously) of seeing how that same critical potential could fuel the rage of the peasant revolt against the starvation caused in part by the same political apparatuses that protected Luther from Rome. However, theologians from other contexts—African-American churches, Asian battlegrounds, and even the frontlines of atheistic theory—would pick up on potential that went beyond Luther's own application. In so doing, though, they were operating within the framework that was nascent in Luther's own theologizing.

With that in mind, after Chapter 2 introduces the basic outlines of Luther's theology of the cross, each subsequent chapter elaborates on a theme hinted at in Luther's work. The key themes are:

- God will never be the same,
- The cross against glory, and
- The community of fidelity to the crucified.

While the final chapter will offer my own constructive theological take on the cross (with my biases and choices no doubt also being apparent throughout), the main goal of the text is to demonstrate that, across the centuries-long and diverse conversation around *theologia crucis*, the above themes not only recur but serve as a catalyst for theologians grounding the critical principles of theology of the cross in the struggles of their own contexts. At stake in these conversations is more than simple justice (although, as we know, even simple justice in our world is often elusive enough); at deeper stake is the question of how these theologians see God operating in the world—in what manner, on whose behalf, and to what end. All Christian theology asserts that God is at work in creation redeeming it to God's ends; however, as we shall see, a consistent theology of the cross trains the theological to seek this work in places where it might seem least likely to be found.

Finally, in order to provide some boundaries to the conversation, we should be clear about what will *not* be included in the scope of this text. For instance, while issues of the mechanics of atonement—that is, theorizing about exactly how the life, death, and resurrection of Christ is salvific for humanity—are inevitable accompaniments to thinking about the cross, this book will not delve deeply into the different models of atonement employed by Christian theologians over the centuries.[8] While these models—e.g., substitutionary atonement, recapitulation, *Christus victor*, etc.—all interact with the theology of the cross in different

8. Readers curious about atonement should consult Schmiechen, *Saving Power.*

ways, the nature of these interactions are best spelled out by considering specific theological examples rather than schematizing their structure in any abstract way. The same goes for historic Christological debates about the mechanics of how the divine and human interact in Jesus.[9]

Similarly, although the resurrection of Jesus Christ (however construed) is both a central tenet of the Christian faith and (as we will see) an indispensable part of any full consideration of the cross, this book will not attempt to cover the various debates and controversies considering the historicity of the resurrection. With few exceptions, every theological strand under consideration here asserts that the power and meaning of the cross is inextricable from the reality of the resurrection—although what "resurrection" actually means might be up for debate. Whether that resurrection is understood to be a literal historical reality or a symbolic one, it cannot be separated from the meaning of the cross. We will deal with the resurrection only in relation to *theologia crucis* specifically and not as a separate topic in its own right.

It should be acknowledged that there is much excellent art—music, painting, sculpture, etc., in both secular and sacred settings—that draws upon the cross of Jesus that to even scratch the surface of that tradition would require a host of companion volumes to this one. For our purposes, the concern in what follows will be texts. While the products of the author's desk may not have the same immediate beauty of those of the artist's bench, thoughts ("logos") matter deeply to theology, and theology (for good or for ill) matters deeply to life. So we will keep our focus there.

My hope is that this guide serves to give some sense of how the trajectory of thinking about the cross inaugurated by Luther (who in turn understood himself to be recovering

9. Cf. Norris, *Christological Controversy*.

some key insights from Paul and the gospel narratives) has blossomed into a host of diverse—and sometimes competing—strategies for doing justice to the scandal of the crucified Messiah and its implications for a world in which the intertwining of suffering, death, and resurrection hope is no less complex than in Jesus' time.

My hope, too, is that there is theological benefit to tarrying with the cross for awhile, to live theologically in the space of Good Friday/Holy Saturday without subsuming them too quickly into Easter morning. One of my favorite pieces of music is the Estonian composer Arvo Pärt's "Passio," a musical rendering of Christ's passion and crucifixion according to St. John. As Orthodox theologian and Pärt scholar Peter Bouteneff notes, the beginning of the piece, the *exordium*, is "a majestic but sorrowful descent in half-note chords . . . and ends on a dissonant sub-dominant, one step short of bringing the scale to its concluding note." However, at the end of the piece, when Christ has died and the choir pleads "You who have suffered for us, have mercy on us!" a transformation occurs: the music shifts to a brighter key, and the piece finally resolves on its eighth (concluding) note of the scale. As Bouteneff writes,

> Theologically speaking, we have been draw into heaven, although as we enter we know well that we could not have come here without having gone through hell. Nor could we have come here without the loving descent of God. Although [Pärt's] *Passio* story never arrives at the resurrection, the victory is won: not by the miracle of Jesus' resurrection, but precisely by his *death*. The death of the divine Son represents the completion of God's entry into the world. All is now filled with God. The True Light has entered every place that was dark, among the living and

> among the dead, "and the darkness did not overcome it" (John 1:5).[10]

While the cross points always to the resurrection, the strange beauty of total incarnation that God's entry into brokenness and injustice represents is its own kind of gospel—one whose news, as we shall see, continues to comfort and to disturb in our own day.

ACKNOWLEDGMENTS

If I am asserting that theology of the cross is an extended conversation across time and space that encompasses multiple contexts and perspectives, then surely writing a book about it is a small taste of that. Special thanks are due to the friends whose conversations about the material here have fueled my interest in this topic and given me insights far beyond what I could have generated on my own: Derek Nelson, Matt Manning, Matthew Myer Boulton, Verity Jones, Vítor Westhelle, Jon Gill, Candice Wassell, Peter Bouteneff, Brian Derrer, Wendy DeBoer, and a host of others whose witness and fidelity to unvarnished reality inspires and challenges me. Elise Erikson Barrett, Callie Smith, Libby Manning, and Brent Hege all did me the great honor of reading and commenting on multiple drafts of the text. Benjamin Taylor helped me with the formatting down the stretch. My teacher Vítor Westhelle, in addition to authoring a number of important studies on the theology of the cross himself, supervised a number of doctoral students who themselves have written compellingly on the theme from their own social and theological locations. I am glad to have this little book stand as my own modest contribution to that literature in his honor. I want to thank,

10. Bouteneff, *Arvo Pärt*, 193–95.

too, Christian Amondson of Syndicate Theology and Chris Spinks of Cascade, as well as all the team at Wipf and Stock, for their great work in helping to see this to print.

Portions of the final chapter were presented as a lecture to the Crossings Community at their 2016 conference in Belleville, Illinois, and I am grateful for the good feedback that I received as well as their permission to reprint sections of that paper. Deep thanks to my colleagues at Christian Theological Seminary in Indianapolis and my community at Christ the Savior Lutheran Church in Fishers, Indiana for providing venues for me to think out loud alongside savvy discussion partners. All thanks in the end goes to my family—Larry and Elizabeth Saler, Mandy and Chad, as well as Mike, Rita, Jeff, and Trent Delliquadri. To my wife Kristen and my children Nora and Cole: thanks for grounding me in reality even as you teach me to hope for more than I otherwise would.

1

LUTHER'S CROSS

WHENEVER MOST THEOLOGIANS THINK of "theology of the cross" today, the name of Martin Luther generally arises first. *Theologia crucis* is a signature motif both within Luther's theology itself and its subsequent legacy upon theology, philosophy, and the church. But it is also heavily contested ground. Luther himself understood the cross to have implications for both religion and politics. And the fact that he weaves both religion and politics together leads to some of the most powerful insights on both of his era.

The interest that Luther's own *theologia crucis* generates in contemporary theologians has kept the power of Luther's theological critiques of human pretension and politically oppressive theology alive. As we will see below, many theologians have used Luther's insights and inspiration to form a theology of the cross that speaks to their contexts. This seems natural: Luther wrote his theology because he was frustrated both with what he took to be the arrogance of theology of his day (which he thought forced God's word into overly systematized and domesticated philosophical categories, derived mostly from Aristotle and Aristotle's Christian heir Thomas Aquinas) and with the power of the church to impose the implications of this theology with unchecked authority. One definition of power is the ability to impose one's fictions on someone else; Luther thought that the power of the church was to impose a fictitious, demanding God upon the people, and benefitting institutionally as a result.

That said, *theologia crucis* for Luther is a not a free-floating theme applicable to any given theological or political project; rather, it is best thought of as a specific theological orientation that allows the ordinary Christian as well as the theologian to live into the fullness of the Christian life in a manner that frees her to engage church tradition, ecclesial structures, and God's word while maintaining the primacy upon God's revelation of grace precisely in the brokenness and dejection of the cross. Luther was not anti-church or anti-government. But for Christians, he thinks that protest is needed when the church replaces the cross with a lust for power.

Likewise, we need to remember the medieval setting of Luther's views on good and evil. Luther's apocalyptic discourse concerning the beleaguered true church and its theology of the cross in opposition to the theology of glory that upholds the false testimony of God's enemies is neither metaphorical nor a stand-in for some more "natural" reality. In the battle between the truth of the cross and the lies of the cross's enemies, Luther understood nothing less than eternal salvation to be at stake, and the stakes remained high for him throughout his life. Whether or not contemporary theologians wish to operate in such dualistic terms, one cannot read Luther without remembering that, for him, perceiving the cross rightly truly is a matter of life and death.

THEOLOGY OF THE CROSS VS. DELUSIONS OF GLORY

This setting within the cosmic drama of judgment, damnation, and salvation helps us to understand the fact that Luther's tendency was to talk less about a given "theology of the cross" and more about a particular kind of stance towards theology as a whole. In Luther's main discussion of the theology of the cross specifically, the 1518 Heidelberg Disputation (written less than a year after the famous posting of the Ninety-five Theses that began Luther's rebellion against his church's selling of indulgences), it is in fact the *theologian* and not theology itself is what Luther is really interested in. The author herself, as much as the texts authored, are at the center of the discussion. This is why the famed theses 19 and 20 of the Heidelberg Disputation discuss, not "theology of the cross" per se, but rather the framework within which the *theologian* of the cross engages both the world and God's revelation. Here are the key theses along with their elaboration:

> (19) That person does not deserve to be called a theologian who looks upon the invisible things of God as though they were clearly perceptible in those which have actually happened [Rom. 1:20]. . . . (20) He deserves to be called a theologian, however, who comprehends the visible and manifest things of God seen through suffering and the cross. . . . Now it is not sufficient for anyone, and it does him no good to recognize God in his glory and majesty, unless he recognizes him in the humility and shame of the cross . . . (21) A theologian of glory calls evil good and good evil. A theologian of the cross calls a thing what it actually is. . . . (22) That wisdom which sees the invisible things of God in

> works as perceived by man is completely puffed up, blinded, and hardened. . . . Because men do not know the cross and hate it, they necessarily love the opposite, namely, wisdom, glory, power, and so on. Therefore the become increasingly blinded and hardened by such love, for desire cannot be satisfied by the acquisition of those things which it desires. . . . Thus also the desire for knowledge is not satisfied by the acquisition of wisdom but is stimulated that much more. (24) Yet that wisdom is not of itself evil, nor is the law to be evaded; but without the theology of the cross man misuses the best in the worst manner.[1]

What does all this mean?

Notice, again, the emphasis is on the person thinking and not the thoughts that are thought. Luther is concerned first and foremost, not with what the theologian says, but with how the theologian's perspective on God and the world is formed. This focus upon the person of the theologian and the optics by which she engages the things of God and the things of the world, as opposed to series of propositions that might be said to make up a "theology of the cross," supports the idea that for Luther the *theologia crucis* is a kind of interpretive lens by which in the tasks of exegesis, theology, and proclamation—and doing so with the goal of chastening the speculative impulse inherent in all these activities.

Chastened by what? By the epistemological and existential limits imposed by the fact that God chooses to be known to the world under the realities of pain, brokenness, and weakness. In other words, for Luther, there is no one set of tenets of propositions that makes up *theologia crucis*;

1. Luther, "Heidelberg Disputation," in *Luther's Works* 31:52–55.

it is more a kind of methodological bearing centered on the theologian's positioning vis-à-vis the scandal of God's choosing to reveal saving truth in the form of brokenness and scandal. The cross gives us lenses to see God that are very different from what is on display in theologies of "glory," those that can only associate God with what is pure, good, and holy.

To be sure, the medieval church in which Luther carried on his work was saturated at both the popular and theological levels with crucifixion imagery. However, Luther's great contribution was to flesh out with unparalleled vigor the notion that the cross must be a formative influence not only upon the content but also the form of thinking about God, and to apply this stricture with rigor and creativity to all aspects of the Christian life. In other words, Luther made the cross a cornerstone of Christian existence in the here and now. As a number of historians have pointed out, the actual term "theology of the cross" comes up often in Luther's early writings, but less in his later work. However, Luther retained and even expanded the substance of the term throughout the remainder of his life and writing career. In fact, careful reading demonstrates that the cross touches everything in Luther's theology—and for Luther, at least, theology touches everything.

As regards Luther's understanding of the cross's role in salvation, his model conforms broadly to what the Christian tradition terms "substitutionary atonement:" in Christ, God takes on the sin of humanity in such a way that those in Christ need no longer bear the punishment that the sin entails. Luther was fond of describing this as a kind of "happy exchange" of the sin of humanity with Christ's perfection—humanity gets the benefit of Christ's perfection even as Christ takes humanity's sins upon himself. However, what has been most influential in Luther's theology of the cross has not been the mechanics of how the cross saves, but rather the critical edge that the cross brings to theological projects that seek to minimize or distort the gospel of God's free gift of grace. That is, for Luther, theologizing about the cross is just as much about deconstructing bad theology as it is about paving the way for better theology.

THEOLOGIA CRUCIS AND THE FORMATION OF THE THEOLOGIAN

The centrality of the cross was present as a theme even in Luther's thinking prior to the Reformation; his sermons between June 1516 and February 1517, immediately prior to the posting of the Theses, contain exhortations to "Preach one thing: the wisdom of the cross!"[2] Later, his "Explanations of the Ninety-Five Theses" (completed in February 1518, amidst Luther's preparation for the debate at which the aforementioned Heidelberg Disputation was presented) makes it clear that the contrast between *theologia crucis* and *theologia gloriae* was not a one-off. It deeply informs how Luther thinks of theology's role in the church:

> Yet in the meantime [the theologians] have opened the floodgates of heaven and flooded the treasury of indulgences and the merits of Christ so that by this deluge almost the whole Christian world is ruined. . . . A theologian of glory does not recognize, along with the Apostle, the crucified and hidden God alone [1 Corinthians 22]. He sees and speaks of God's glorious manifestation among the heathen, how the invisible nature can be known from the things which are visible, and how he is present and powerful in all things everywhere. . . . Yet the theologian of

2. Luther, "Early Sermons," in *Luther's Works* 51:15, 17ff.

> glory still receives money for his treasury, while the theologian of the cross, on the other hand, offers the merits of Christ freely. Yet people do not consider the theologian of the cross worthy of consideration, but finally even persecute him.[3]

Following the logic of this passage, we can envision how the target of *theologia crucis*' critical edge, as wielded by Luther, was a kind of theo-political edifice. The edifice was comprised of the mutually reinforcing achievements of the church's theology and the economic/political power of the Roman church. "For Luther understands the cross of Christ in a quite unmystical way as God's protest against the misuse of [God's] name for the purpose of a religious consummation of human wisdom, human works and the Christian imperialism of medieval ecclesiastical society."[4] For Luther the theologian, the church's abuses of power were inextricable from what he took to be the theological errors of his day: interpreting theology through philosophical categories (particularly Aristotle) and over-confidence in what humans can know about God's nature.[5]

More specifically, according to Luther, both the church in its sale of indulgences *and* scholastic theology in its indebtedness to philosophical categories foreign to the gospel located the things of God in the true, the good, and beautiful in such a way as to privilege that which is powerful and successful on earth. As Mary Solberg writes,

> The moralism and religious intellectualism of the church and the scholastic method [of theology] both reflected and fostered something Luther

3. Luther, "Explanations of the 95 Theses," in *Luther's Works* 31:227.

4. Moltmann, *Crucified God*, 208.

5. Cf. Ruge-Jones, *Cross in Tensions*.

> understood as even more basic, something he targeted over and over again in his theologizing. Humans, he contended, believe and act as if they have the power to invent, name, describe, control, and dispense God. This god, however, is a god of their own choosing, bearing no resemblance to God who creates and redeems them by a power that is God's alone. The god humans invent can be found whenever (human) glory, majesty, and power are most evident, whether on the scale of the institutional church or of the individual human heart.[6]

In other words, theology of glory is idolatry at the level of both individual piety and institutional power.

One of the biggest problems with theologians of glory, on this account, is that they erase what Luther took to be the most fundamental reversal of human wisdom perpetrated by the gospel: "God can be found only in suffering and the cross."[7] Think of the biblical examples: while Jesus' disciples looked for a messiah who could overthrow Rome, they got a broken criminal executed in humiliating fashion. Instead of fashioning the church from the elite of the day, God (according to Paul and the early disciples) chose slaves, peasants, and other disempowered people to comprise the church. Thus, Luther understood his staurocentrism as aligning with a deeply biblical pattern.

His *theologia crucis*, then, is a mode of comprehending the world and God's actions within it, but this comprehension has a critical edge aimed at resisting and dismantling the marriage between two kinds of arrogance: theology unchastened by the cross and a church that has located obedience to God's will in earthly success rather than fidelity

6. Solberg, *Compelling Knowledge*, 74.

7. Luther, "Heidelberg Disputation," in *Luther's Works* 31:53.

to the crucified Messiah (as exemplified in this case by the indulgence controversy that prompted Luther's original protest against his own church). Bad thinking about God leads to exploitative churches built in God's name.

We have said that Luther points towards *theologia crucis* as representing an entire orientation for the theologian, an orientation in which accurate knowledge of God's work in the world takes the incarnation as both the starting point and, to a certain extent, the boundary for speculative inquiry. Speculation about God begins and ends with the cross. The concern here is a kind of theological epistemology; that is, not only what theologians know, but how they go about knowing it. As Gerhard Ebeling points out,

> The knowledge of God which is given in Jesus Christ does not therefore constitute a particular item of doctrine which supplements a general knowledge of God, but is the beginning of all true knowledge of God and man. It is the complete opposite of speculation concerning God in his nakedness, God in his majesty, and points us toward God who came in the flesh and was therefore clothed in promises, who came close to us, imparted himself to us, and was thereby revealed.[8]

The theologian of the cross clings to God's revelation as opposed to speculating about that which remains hidden in God. Strikingly, though, this methodological stricture implies that the theologian herself must be subject to persecution—both because her resolute focus on seeing God's

8. Ebeling, *Luther,* 223. We should note here that, for Luther, the "cross" refers not simply to the crucifixion of Jesus of Nazareth but to the entire shape of the incarnation: Jesus' entire life, death, and resurrection, including its prefigurement in God's dealings with Israel in the Old Testament.

presence in that which the world despises will subject her to ridicule, and because (as noted above) the gospel proclamation that stems from *theologia crucis* threatens the interests of worldly powers (which Luther ultimately understood to be in thrall to demonic forces oppressing the true church). While focus on the cross always runs the risk of what the Christian tradition has called "dolorism"—that is, focusing on the suffering of Christ or oneself with unhealthy fixation, as if one is reveling in it—it is true that Luther thinks that Christians suffering for the right reason is an inevitable part of Christian life in a world set against God.

SUFFERING AND THE CHRISTIAN LIFE

But if *theologia crucis* is about the life of the theologian, then what does that life look like? Indeed, when he was writing about the qualities that make up an effective and faithful theologian, Luther famously argued that, in addition to prayer and contemplation, the true theologian also must suffer the attacks of *tentatio*. What is that? More than simple "temptation," *tentatio* is best thought of as deeply personal "soul attacks" that might allow the devil to convince the believer that the gospel is not true for her. While the immediate context of this *Anfechtung*, or "struggle," is attacks upon the believer's existential being by the devil, in the broader context of Luther's ecclesiology it is clear that the persecution suffered by the true theologian is itself part of the formation by which correct perception and proclamation of the gospel can happen.[9] As von Loewenich writes, "'Cross's and 'suffering' refer, in the first place, to Christ's suffering and cross. But Luther is thinking at the same time

9. Luther, "Preface to the Wittenberg Edition," in *Luther's Works* 34:285ff.

about the cross of the Christian. For Luther the cross of Christ and the cross of the Christian belong together."[10]

The logic here is this: the speculations of a theologian who herself has not undergone "the cross" in the form of *tentatio/Anfechtung* are suspect precisely because the theologian who is *not* suffering is too friendly with the powers that oppress real truth. Theology shows us that engagement with God's truth as God reveals it has consequences. This is both because God's word is hostile to the principalities and powers of "glory," and because God chooses for truth itself to be found in that which the world despises. True theology is written from a place of endurance because suffering is inevitable for Christians who follow Christ in the world.

That is why theology of the cross cannot finally be separated from the total life of the Christian: for Luther, the only way for the Christian to ward off despair and to see gospel in that which is abject from the world's perspective is for her to be sustained on a continual basis by sound preaching, the sacraments rightly administered, immersion in God's word, prayer, etc. The Christian life properly practiced brings the believer to the cross repeatedly, but it also sustains the soul battered by *tentatio* such that the sweetness of the gospel can provide courage for the task of theology, and indeed Christian living as a whole. This, more so than any consciousness of God feeling wrath against the sinner, is what Luther sees at the heart of Christian life: gratitude for the salvation that God gives in Christ fueling a life of love lived out in the world.

Finally, all of this for Luther has to do with the question of justification: in what ways does Christ make us righteous? For Luther theology of glory necessarily leads to the impossible demands of works righteousness: if God's grace is to be found in the beautiful, successful, and powerful

10. Von Loewenich, *Luther's Theology of the Cross*, 20.

things of this world—and indeed, even in the justice and virtues of this world—then correspondingly the sinner will be expected to bring good works to the cooperative venture of salvation. However, if *theologia crucis* reverses the world's expectations of what righteousness looks like and teaches the sinner to look for God's salvific action precisely in the most abject places of death within the gospel narratives and within the world itself, then the cross stands at the center of proper preaching about justification. To be sure, Luther understood that there is a sense in which Christ's death on the cross saves the Christian from God's judgment on the Last Day; however, meditation on this fact is meant to train the Christian to encounter God's grace more thoroughly.

As Luther puts it, "This is the love of the cross, born of the cross, which turns in the direction where it does not find good which it may enjoy, but where it may confer good upon the bad and needy person."[11] It is the abject sinner that God chooses to justify through the life, death, and resurrection of Jesus Christ. This, by the way, is why Luther famously regarded any sort of cooperative view of salvation (in which humans work alongside God in securing their own salvation) as nullifying the cross: because it presumes a partial rather than thoroughgoing transformation of our natural tendency to self-justify. As Luther would put it:

> This is clear: He who does not know Christ does not know God hidden in suffering. Therefore he prefers works to suffering, glory to the cross, strength to weakness, wisdom to folly, and, in general, good to evil. These are the people whom the apostle calls "enemies of the cross of Christ" (Phil. 3:18), for they hate the cross and suffering and love works and the glory of works. Thus they call the good of the cross evil and the

11. Luther, "Heidelberg Disputation," in *Luther's Works* 31:57.

> evil of a deed good. God can be found only in suffering and the cross, as has already been said. Therefore the friends of the cross say that the cross is good and works are evil, for through the cross works are dethroned and the old Adam, who is especially edified by works, is crucified. It is impossible for a person not to be puffed up by his good works unless he has first been deflated and destroyed by suffering and evil until he knows that he is worthless and that his works are not his but God's.[12]

Ultimately, the cross is about God's resurrecting of Jesus creating righteousness where it is least likely to be found. And for Luther, the righteousness given in Christ is synonymous with life abundant. The tie between Good Friday and Easter, then, is not the latter entirely dispensing with the former but rather the cross giving shape to the mode of God's creating life in the face of death. In other words, the cross is how God acts in the world as much as it is humanity's attempted rejection of that action. That this rejection does not stymie God's redemptive work is the crux of Luther's view that God justifies us when we cannot justify ourselves, and that God creates life in places of death. As Fleming Rutledge writes,

> Christians do not simply look to the cross of Christ with prayerful reverence. We are set in motion by its power, energized by it, upheld by it, guaranteed by it, secured by it for the promised future because it is the power of the creating Word that "gives life to the dead and calls into existence the things that do not exist" (Rom 4:17).[13]

12. Ibid., 53.

13. Rutledge, *Crucifixion*, 14.

LUTHER'S LEGACY

We have spent so much time on Luther because, as we will see in the next chapters, while contemporary theologies of the cross tend to dispose with certain dated aspects of Luther's thought (including, fortunately, his bad habit of identifying his ecclesial and political opponents with the minions of Satan), his theology of the cross lays the groundwork for much of what would be taken up by his theological heirs. The cross of Christ impacts how we think about God, and that in turn impacts how we think about the structures that speak in the name of truth, beauty, and justice. The shifting sands of how God-talk, politics, and justice interrelate make up the different contexts in which *theologia crucis* has been employed since Luther's time; however, all of these strands can be said to follow the basic pattern established by Luther. And that pattern is this: when one speaks of the cross rightly, then it brings us into conflict with those principalities and powers that would use a "God of glory" to give aid and comfort to structures of exploitation. Luther's cross deconstructs God-talk in the name of fidelity to the gospel and in pursuit of justice. This sets the stage for all that is to come.

Questions

1. Based on what you have read in this chapter, what about Luther's worldview seems dated ("stuck in the past," tied to his medieval context but not applicable to ours), and what seems helpful in our own time?
2. Do you agree that the Christian life entails suffering if it is done right?
3. Where do you see theology and power collaborating towards injustice in our own time? Towards justice?

Suggestions for further reading:

For a comprehensive and readable biography of Luther's life, see Timothy Lull and Derek Nelson, *Resilient Reformer: The Life and Thought of Martin Luther* (Minneapolis: Fortress, 2015). Walter Von Loewenich, *Luther's Theology of the Cross*; 5th ed., trans. H.J.A. Bouman (Minneapolis: Augsburg, 1976) remains the best sustained argument for the idea that the theology of the cross is a key motif throughout Luther's life and not just his early writings. For an argument that Luther is particularly daring in his formulation of God's suffering on the cross, see Dennis Ngien, *The Suffering of God According to Luther's Theologa Crucis* (Vancouver: Regent College Publishing, 1995); however, for a recent counterargument against the idea that Luther broke radically from medieval notions about God's lack of suffering on the cross, see David Luy, *Dominus Mortis: Martin Luther on the Incorruptibility of God in Christ* (Minneapolis: Fortress, 2014). For an excellent examination of the political and social implications of Luther's theology of the cross, see Philip Ruge-Jones, *Cross in Tensions: Luther's Theology of the Cross as Theologico-Social Critique* (Eugene, OR: Pickwick, 2008). For a reading of Luther on the cross that tries to establish rapport with more feminist readings (as we will discuss in Chapter 3), see Deanna A. Thompson, *Crossing the Divide: Luther, Feminism, and the Cross* (Minneapolis: Augsburg Fortress, 2004).

2

GOD WILL NEVER BE THE SAME

The theology of the cross—as exemplified in Luther, in Kierkegaard, in the early Barth, in Tillich, in Jürgen Moltmann and Elisabeth Moltmann-Wendel, in Alan Lewis, in Mary Solberg, and in many others—by no means minimizes Jesus' representation of God. But since its sees this representation under the guise of what is opposite to deity as commonly conceived, it maintains throughout a strong hold on the real humanity of Christ. It understands this unique representation of God as occurring hiddenly through this genuinely human life.[1]

To SAY THAT THE theology of the cross necessitates that "God will never be the same" makes the most sense when we remember that "theology" refers first and foremost, not

1. Hall, *Cross in Our Context*, 124.

to the truth about God *per se*, but rather human words ("logos") *about* God. The "God" present in any given theology is thus, by necessity, a moving target. Indeed, in our explication of Luther's theology of the cross in the last chapter, we saw that it is no exaggeration to say that what is at stake between the theology of the cross and theology of glory is a fight between two very different "Gods:" one who is present most directly in that which the world calls good and powerful, and one who is hidden under the contradiction (*sub contrario*, as Luther would say) of weakness and death. This is not to say that theology of the cross is anti-beauty; however, to understand God present in the world's brokenness deeply modifies what our concept of beauty might be (more on this in Chapter 4).

Thus, when we speak of an epistemology of the cross as it relates to God and the world, we get to one of the truly vital centers not only of Luther's thought, but of all subsequence *theologia crucis* since his time: when one places the cross of the crucified Messiah at the center of "God-talk," then the image of God that emerges cannot remain unscathed, unchastened, unaltered by the event of Jesus Christ. Put differently, *theologia crucis* understands Jesus' life, death, and resurrection to be an event in the life of God that must impact all subsequent theologizing about the divine and God's relationship to a suffering world.

We will see in the next chapter how this is applied to ethics by a host of theologians seeking a critical principle for deconstructing death-dealing theologies in their various contexts; in this chapter, though, we will see how images of God themselves have undergone transformation within the last century on the basis of the growing prominence of *theologia crucis* within the theological scene.

THE ECLIPSE AND RETURN OF THE CROSS

One of the most striking things about Luther's theology of the cross is how thoroughly it disappeared from the theological scene, even within Luther's own lifetime. Once the Reformation itself began to take on momentum, Luther's own theology began to be secondary in importance to the confessional documents that the movement as a whole would come to ratify (such as the Augsburg Confession); moreover, as historians have pointed out, the Reformation as experienced on the ground by the average sixteenth-century European was the so-called "Radical" Reformation, not the exchange of sophisticated theological formulations that characterized the action in the universities and imperial courts.[2] Indeed, Luther's own theological legacy would quickly be eclipsed until the rediscovery of Luther during the renaissance in Luther studies that took place in early twentieth-century Germany.

That rediscovery coincided with other factors that contributed to theologians' interest in recovering a theological basis for understanding God at work amidst death and failure. To understand this, however, a bit more background is needed.

As is well known, the period following the Reformation in Europe was wracked with violence. The religious uncertainty caused both by the debates between the Reformers and the Roman Catholic church and by the splintering of "Protestantism" into various competing factions (Anabaptists, Calvinist, etc.) was exacerbated by tensions surrounding emerging national identities in Germany and elsewhere. The combination produced a great deal of violence, both on the battlefields of Europe and in churches

2. Cf. Gregory, *Unintended Reformation.*

whose accoutrements of medieval Christian worship (icons, rood screens, etc.) might be smashed or looted.

As a number of scholars have pointed out, the intellectual movement that became known (in various forms) as the European Enlightenment—heralding the onset of the transition from the late medieval to the modern period—had sociological reasons for privileging the use of rationality as opposed to loyalty to past authorities (including the church). The Enlightenment cry *Sapere aude*! ("Have the courage to use your own reason!") on this account was less a matter of intellectual hubris on the part of philosophically sophisticated academics and was more a plea for an end to violence and bloodshed that philosophers and others increasingly saw as the result of blind obedience to claims of revelation and authority that could not be verified by independent reason.[3]

While intellectual movements such as Romanticism would come to challenge the Enlightenment's confidence in human rationality, the general thrust of Western intellectual history leading from the Reformation into the nineteenth century was one of general optimism in the advance of humanity—including advances in theology. The father of modern liberal theology, Friedrich Schleiermacher (1768–1834), thought that the Christian faith in his time was in a position to jettison stale doctrinal formulations that no longer spoke to the modern age; meanwhile, his philosophical contemporary, Georg Wilhelm Friedrich Hegel (1770–1831), increasingly interpreted the progress of human thought (including religion) as inevitable and heading towards greater peacefulness and prosperity. Such cognate movements as Deism (broadly the notion that God creates a rationally ordered universe but then does not intervene in it further) and the theories of doctrinal development

3. Cf. Toulmin, *Cosmopolis*.

offered by both Protestant and Catholic modernist theologians served to further this general atmosphere of opposing science/reason to "irrational" truths that could only be taken on faith as revealed.

In such an atmosphere, the theology of the cross (to the extent that it was even mentioned) would have several strikes against its appeal. The notion that God might be so arbitrary as to act in irrational fashion, enacting salvation through the sufferings of an executed Messiah, was a bad fit with optimism in the powers of human reason and development. More damningly, its irrationality might well have raised the spectre of a return to religious authoritarianism (since such spectres always accompany demands to subsume human reason under theological claims, especially those made by churches).

However, if the nineteenth century was one of historical optimism in theology, then it all came crashing to a halt at the onset of the twentieth century—a century that has a claim to being, in the West at least, one of the most savage and bloody in the human record. Not only were two world wars fought, but the conditions under which the first was conducted (including the introduction of such horrors as trench warfare and mustard gas) and the second was waged (culminating, of course, in the utter brutality of the Holocaust) rendered the optimism of the nineteenth century worse than laughable. The twentieth-century theologian Paul Tillich spoke for most of his generation when he remarked that he had learned his theology in the trenches (of WWI, in his case).

The utter failure of facile notions of "progress" (theological and otherwise) gave particular impetus to the twentieth century's return to pre-modern sources, including Luther, in an attempt to rediscover the power of symbols such as sin, death, guilt, God's shattering of human reason, etc.—symbols that made little sense in the wake of the Enlightenment but were suddenly needed to make sense of a world that had seemingly gone insane.

THE CROSS AT THE CENTER, AND THE CENTER AT THE MARGINS

Straddling the line between nineteenth-century optimism and the political breakdowns of the twentieth century was Dietrich Bonhoeffer (1906–1945).[4] The promising young German student's theological education took place at the University of Berlin, where a number of the finest theological minds associated with the previous century's theological optimism were his teachers. Outside of their classes, however, Bonhoeffer was falling under the theological influence of thinkers whose skepticism about such optimism (such as the Swiss theologian Karl Barth) was leading them to recover unfashionably "pre-modern" doctrines such as atonement, original sin, divine inspiration of the Bible, etc. Additional travels to the United States, in which the relatively facile theological offerings of classical Protestant liberalism failed to make sense both of the aftermath of World War I and the ongoing systemic racism that Bonhoeffer saw across the American South, further solidified his sense that classical theological themes of sin, judgment, and the inbreaking of God's kingdom were needed in order to name the chaos of reality well.

Upon his return to Germany, circumstances would quickly force the moment of crisis. As the Third Reich came to power and the University of Berlin (where Bonhoeffer was now himself lecturing) became Nazified, Bonhoeffer left the academy in order to pursue the ministry, first as an ecumenical liaison, and eventually as the principal

4. Cf. Marsh, *Strange Glory.*

of an illegal seminary—Finkenwalde—associated with the "Confessing Church" that rose up in opposition to the Third Reich's growing control of the established churches of Germany.

Famously, upon being convinced by his brother-in-law (who had a position with German military intelligence) of the extent of Nazi crimes against Jews and others, Bonhoeffer served as an advisor and spy to a movement that attempted to subvert the Nazi influence upon Germany, up to and including attempts to assassinate Hitler. Bonhoeffer was arrested in 1943, initially on relatively minor charges of evading German military service and minor conspiracy against the Third Reich; however, when his role in the unsuccessful assassination attempt was discovered, he was executed in 1945 (immediately prior to Germany's surrender and the end of the war).

Despite his relatively brief time in the academy proper, Bonhoeffer remained an active theological writer all of his life; moreover, particularly as the political situation in Germany deteriorated, his writings tended to emphasize—in conscious opposition to the liberalism of his day—what his mentor Barth called the "strange new world" of the Bible and its demands upon the Christian. While Bonhoeffer was never a fundamentalist or a biblical literalist, he became fascinated with the prospect that the Bible and the church mediate the living Christ to humanity, and do it in categories that force disciples of Christ to reorient themselves towards that which is countercultural and strange.

While in prison, Bonhoeffer wrote a series of treatises and letters to his family, but also to his friend and close theological collaborator, Eberhard Bethge. He reflected on the experience of the church in his time, and what being subjected to the rise of the Third Reich (with its indictment of the church's failure to resist) might mean:

> There remains an experience of incomparable value. We have for once learnt to see the great events of world history from below, from the perspective of the outcast, the suspects, the maltreated, the powerless, the oppressed, the reviled—in short, from the perspective of those who suffer. The important thing is neither that bitterness nor envy should have gnawed at the heart during this time, that we should have come to look with new eyes at matters great and small, sorrow and joy, strength and weakness, that our perception of generosity, humanity, justice and mercy should have become clearer, freer, less corruptible. We have to learn that personal suffering is a more effective key, a more rewarding principle for exploring the world in thought and action than personal good fortune. This perspective from below must not become the partisan possession of those who are eternally dissatisfied; rather, we must do justice to life in all its dimensions from a higher satisfaction, whose foundation is beyond any talk of "from below" or "from above." This is the way in which we may affirm it.[5]

Like Luther, Bonhoeffer saw the task of Christian faithfulness going forward as implying a kind of epistemology, or way of knowing the world. Hitler had risen to power partly on the basis of promises to restore the church to the center of the moral life of Germany, to move the institutional church back to its former position of glory. Aristocratic families like Bonhoeffer's had largely capitulated to the lure of this promise.

However, while in prison, Bonhoeffer began formulating the promise of what he famously called "religionless

5. Bonhoeffer, *Letters and Papers*, 52.

Christianity," one in which the gospel would be carried forward without the trappings or security of institutional religion. Much ink has been spilled on these enigmatic passages from Bonhoeffer, and the simple truth is that he did not live long enough to fully flesh out his thoughts on them. However, what is clear is that Bonhoeffer's view of what it might mean for Christians to engage the world from the margins rather than at the center of society was tied to his theology of the cross. "God consents to be pushed out of the world and onto the cross; God is weak and powerless in the world and in precisely this way, and only so, is at our side and helps us."[6]

For Bonhoeffer, God as conceived within the standard "religion" of his day is a kind of supernatural add-on to human life that seeks to take human beings out of deep immersion in the cares and trials of their day in order to give a kind of illusory comfort—one that, in the face of a world seemingly gone insane under the horrors of the Third Reich, as well as (somewhat paradoxically) with the growing independence of post-Enlightenment humanity from any need of supernatural explanations in order to make sense of the world, was quickly becoming either obsolete or idolatrous. God is becoming less necessary; however, this reveals to us that the "necessary" God always was an idol. The God who chooses to be known in the broken man on the cross is a God who does not seek to supplement normal human existence, but to turn it upside down. This happens, though, not by a religious removal from the world, but by deeper immersion into reality in all its ambiguity. The cross drives us deeper into reality as such—and deep into reality is where God chooses to be found in Christ.

Indeed, without stretching the analogy too far, we might indeed say that, for Bonhoeffer, the parallels between

6. Ibid., 479.

"religion" in the classic sense and Luther's "theology of glory" are evident. In his day, Bonhoeffer saw the hold of "religion" a kind of cultic piety separated from the concerns of the daily world to be less and less appealing to those struggling in the world, *even as* the existential and material concerns to which the gospel of Jesus Christ addresses itself remain more real than ever. Bonhoeffer's "religionless Christianity," then, is a move past the separation of the church from the world that misses the fact that the crucified Christ is a signpost precisely for how deeply God chooses to go into the world. The church of religion, for Bonhoeffer, is a church that refuses to be as incarnate—as deep into the world—as the God that it worships. To be deep into the world as Christ is, though, is to be in the world as a people willing to be crucified, marginalized, and even—as Bonhoeffer was—martyred for obedience to the call of Christ to be against the forces of death.

In light of our historical survey above, what is particularly striking about Bonhoeffer's case is that it demonstrates that, even as the Enlightenment sought to leave a God of "superstition" or "supernaturalism" behind, the God of human reason that remained was insufficient to speak to the horrors of the twentieth century (or, we might say, the horrors felt throughout by those—enslaved Africans in the United States, for instance—not in a position to benefit from the supposed fruits of nineteenth-century optimism). As a theologian, Bonhoeffer offers his theology of the cross, not simply as an ethical program for Christians going forward, but as a significant reconceptualizing of God and God's relationship to the world. "Only a suffering God can help."[7]

7. Ibid., 479.

In other words, what is at stake in theology of the cross is nothing less than God, and how we speak of God. All ethics proceeds from this.

A GOD WHO SUFFERS?

The theologian arguably most responsible for revitalizing *theologia crucis* in the twentieth century was himself on the front lines of the same horrors as Bonhoeffer. The German theologian Jürgen Moltmann first discovered the study of theology while a prisoner of war from 1945–48. Upon becoming a professional theologian, he remained drawn to the study, not only of Luther, but of other twentieth-century theologians and philosophers for whom the notion of the cross and hope remains central.

In a striking passage in his 1973 text *The Crucified God*, Moltmann recounts a scene from Elie Wiesel's novel *Night*, in which a Jewish youth is being hung agonizingly in a Nazi concentration camp:

> The SS hanged two Jewish men and a youth in front of the whole camp. The men died quickly, but the death throes of the youth lasted for half an hour. "Where is God? Where is he?" someone asked behind me. As the youth hung still in torment in the noose after a long time, I heard the man call again, "Where is God now?" And I heard a voice in myself answer, "Where is he? He is here. He is hanging there on the gallows . . ."

Moltmann goes on to comment:

> Any other answer would be blasphemy. There cannot be any other Christian answer to the question of this torment. To speak here of a God

> who could not suffer would make God a demon. To speak here of an absolute God would make God an annihilating nothingness. To speak here of an indifferent God would condemn men to indifference.[8]

Moltmann's target, that which he calls a "demonic" theology, is the notion that God in Godself cannot suffer. To be sure, Christian theologians from the beginning had acknowledged that, to the extent that Jesus is truly God (affirmed by the church's rejection of the heresy of Ebionism, among others) and truly human (rejecting Docetism), then of course it can be said that the divine suffers on the cross. However, in rejecting too the heresy of patripassionism ("Father-suffering"), the church also signaled its unease with the notion that God in Godself can have *pathos*—that is, suffer in the way that creatures suffer (this is where we get the word "pathetic," for instance). Such might imply a kind of lack in God that would, in the mind of the early church fathers, be problematic if we also say that God creates and sustains the world while existing as perfect love.[9] Thus, most orthodox Christian theology had said that, while God suffers as the second person of the Trinity in Christ, God in Godself does not suffer.

For Moltmann, this notion confuses the gospel of Jesus Christ—which, again, posits a God who is willing to be incarnate deeply into the world, including its sufferings—with a God more akin to that of pre-Christian philosophy. For the most part, it was a commonplace of Greek metaphysical traditions especially that divinity and suffering are incompatible, since suffering implies change and the divine was generally considered to be timeless and unchangeable.

8. Moltmann, *Crucified God*, 273–74.

9. For a careful and nuanced survey of patristic attitudes on God's suffering, cf. Gavrilyuk, *Suffering of the Impassible God*.

However, Moltmann credits Luther and his daring invocations of the suffering of the divine on the cross (along with Luther's radicalization of the notion that of the "communication of attributes" between the different persons of the Trinity, in which we can say that whatever happens to the Father happens also to the Son, and so on) with breaking through this barrier and allowing for a Christian grammar of divine suffering that affects the entirety of God's being, not only Jesus. For Moltmann, Luther's *theologia crucis* "made it possible to conceive of God himself in the god-forsakenness of Christ and to ascribe suffering and death on the cross to the divine-human person of Christ. If this divine nature in the person of the eternal Son of God is the centre which creates a person in Christ, then it too suffered and died."[10] Just as Bonhoeffer thinks that only a suffering God can help humanity, Moltmann thinks that only a suffering God is truly biblical if we see the cross of Christ as the center of the gospel. "The death of Christ reaches deep into the nature of God and, above all other meanings, is an event that takes place in the innermost nature of God, the Trinity."[11]

This suffering is Trinitarian for Moltmann. The Son, Jesus Christ, suffers the pain of crucifixion, whereas the Father suffers the pain of the parent experiencing the death of the child. The Spirit, as the bond of love that sustains both the Father/Son relationship and humanity's connection to this event, redounds with the same suffering as well.

In Moltmann's view, a God who truly suffers is a God who has entered fully enough into the human experience that full solidarity with the human experience is possible. Although Moltmann could be read (as he sometimes in fact is) as arguing that God somehow would not know what it

10. Moltmann, *Crucified God* 234.

11. Moltmann, "Crucified God, Yesterday and Today," 133.

would be like to suffer as a human without the experience of Christ, a more charitable interpretation would be to take it along the same lines as Luther and Bonhoeffer: God's suffering on the cross shows how "all in" God is on the incarnation. There is no divine reserve that somehow merits the name God that exists at a distance from the very God and very man—Jesus Christ—who suffers on the cross. God suffers on the cross, not out of curious desire to know what it feels like to suffer as a human, but out of loving desire to be in absolute and full solidarity with the human experience.

Whether or not one agrees with Moltmann that the theology of the cross necessitates that we understand God in Godself suffering (and not every self-identified theologian of the cross does agree with that proposition), like Bonhoeffer, Moltmann draws out what we might call the "combat theology" aspects of *theologia crucis*: it is against certain gods. Just as Luther is opposed to a god of "glory" whose demand for human works-righteousness aided and abetted the construction of oppressive political and church structures, and Bonhoeffer is opposed to a god who simply serves as the religious supplement to the status quo, Moltmann is arguing that not all Christian conceptions of God are worthy of the name. We might put the matter this way: there are multiple conceptions of God to which atheism is superior.

CURSING AT THE CROSS

We saw from Luther that a key tenet of the theology of the cross is that bad theology leads to bad church; that is, oppressive conceptions of God forms the backbone of exploitative or misguided ecclesial practices. As theologian Douglas John Hall has argued, following Bonhoeffer's lead, it may be that the sort of theology of the cross that attacks the god of triumphalist theology has implications for a church that, in the North American and European contexts at least, has lost its status as cultural broker of society's morals but is, as a result, free to pursue the countercultural path of the cross to be among those that society deems disreputable or weak.[12]

When I was growing up, for instance, in my small, rural town it was generally understood that the church was an institution that partnered with other institutions—schools, government, etc.—to serve the moral order of the town. Even those who did not attend church generally respected the church as a broker of respectability; hence, the understanding that children would be brought to church in order to learn to be "good" (with "good" being defined largely by cultural conformity, no matter how robustly we might sing "Lift High the Cross" when Lent came!). However, as secularization hits even the Bible Belt and multiple contenders for teaching basic morality begin to replace the church, churches there are faced with the same choice that faced the early church: will the church seek to continue to hold on to the fading glory of memories of cultural capital, or will they embrace their status as communities in which is precisely those who are on the outskirts of respectability and worldly success can find a word of salvation addressed to them? There is certainly no shortage of poverty, brokenness, and injustice in communities such as the one that I grew up in. Will the churches there be churches of glory or churches of the cross?

A striking illustration of this principle in action is found in a somewhat unlikely place: a Hollywood teen comedy, albeit one with religion in the backdrop. The satirical movie *Saved!* is a kind of genre exercise: a classic teen movie (that even has its climax at the senior prom) that somewhat

12. Hall, *Cross in Our Context.*

subversively tackles some of the same questions asked by the theologians in this chapter: what sort of God-imagery fosters justice and connection rather than exploitation and injustice in a fallen world, particularly in churches?

In the movie, teenager Mary Cummings, who is a born-again Evangelical Christian attending American Eagle Christian High School along with her two best friends Hilary Faye and Veronica, are part of a girl group named the "Christian Jewels." Hilary Faye is the ringleader of the group who leverages her visible (perhaps too-visible) piety into popularity at the school. Mary's work, however, is more frayed. Her boyfriend Dean comes out to her as gay, which in the worldview of the school is a terrible sin (and a lifestyle choice). In a last-ditch and misguided attempt to "cure" him, Mary seduces him in hopes that she will be doing God's will in helping him to enjoy sex with a woman. However, Dean is sent away to faith-based reparative therapy anyway (Mercy House, which, as one character points out, is less for the troubled youth who are sent there and more "for the people doing the sending").

Mary tells her friends, as well as Hilary's brother Roland (who is a skeptic, partly because of his having been paralyzed in an accident as a youth) about Dean's homosexuality, and makes them promise to keep it a secret. Roland, meanwhile, is attracted to a Jewish girl who is openly disdainful of the school's phony politics of piety, Cassandra Edelstein. When Mary discovers that she is pregnant with Dean's baby from their ill-fated encounter, however, her faith in God's goodness is challenged; in a key scene, she stands in front of a large wooden banner of Jesus and swears with previously forbidden curse words, ending in "God damn." Mary eventually drifts away from Hilary Faye and her Christian friends in favor of hanging out with Roland

and Cassandra, who support her in her pregnancy even as she keeps it a secret from her Christian friends and mother.

As the movie progresses, its discourse about God and religion progresses on two increasingly separate tracks. On the one hand (and to a perhaps stereotypical degree), the most openly pious and institutionally Christian students such as Hilary Faye prove to be nasty, unmerciful, and judgmental—all the stereotypes of evangelical Christians that one might expect from a mainstream Hollywood teen comedy. However, the track that Mary and the other protagonists (such as the skeptic Roland and the secular Jew Cassandra) follow is not atheistic—indeed, as the movie ends with reconciliation and the motley crew of various "rejects" from American Eagle Christian school joined together in a hospital marveling at the birth of Mary's baby, the film makes it clear that the characters themselves have not abandoned God, but replaced their previously toxic and institutionally "blessed" God-imagery (rife as it was with certainty, clear insider-outsider dynamics, and an ethos of escape from the secular world) with a theology that embraces uncertainty and grey areas.

Indeed, what emerges at the end of *Saved!* is, on my reading, nothing other than a church—a community of fragile, broken people whose skepticism about the theology that funds the institutions that have oppressed them cannot overcome their lingering sense that God is at work at the margins of respectability—including religious respectability! It is, perhaps unwittingly, a striking depiction of what the church of a crucified savior might look like.

An even more penetrating example of this is found in the classic novel *Silence* by Japanese Roman Catholic theologian Shusaku Endo. In the novel, a Portuguese Jesuit missionary, Sebastião Rodrigues undergoes hardship while traveling to Japan in 1639 to find a mentor who has supposedly apostatized in the face of persecution by the Japanese government against the church.

To find hidden Christians, security officials were in the habit of testing suspected Christians by forcing them to trample on a *fumie*, a crudely carved image of Christ. Those who refuse are imprisoned and killed by being hung upside down over a foul pit and slowly bled to death.

Rodrigues sustains himself in this mission by focusing on what he takes to be the glory of being martyred for the faith; simultaneous with this, he focuses in on the "beautiful" face of Christ for succor for this potential death. And indeed, Rodrigues and Garrpe are eventually captured and forced to watch as Japanese Christians are martyred. However, to Rodrigues's growing dismay, there is in fact no glory in these pitiful deaths—they are cruel and seemingly pointless. In his prayers, he increasingly experiences God, not as beautiful or meaningful, but as silent in the face of this suffering.

At a key moment during his capture, Rodrigues finds out that his mentor who has apostatized did so in order to save Christians who were being hung in the pit and left to die unless he trampled the *fumie*. Rodrigues, meanwhile, also hears the moans of those who have recanted but are being tortured until Rodrigues does the same. His beautiful Christ is of no avail; he feels abandoned.

However, when Rodrigues looks upon a *fumie*, he hears Christ breaks his silence:

> You may trample. You may trample. I more than anyone know of the pain in your foot. You may trample. It was to be trampled on by men that I was born into this world. It was to share men's pain that I carried my cross.[13]

13. Endo, *Silence*, 171.

Hearing this, Rodrigues tramples and apostatizes; in doing so, he gives up on all the supposed glory awaiting martyrs who persevere in the faith until the end. The reader is left uncertain as to whether this gesture on Rodrigues's part is justified.

When framed within the terms of the theology of the cross, though, Rodrigues's action takes on a powerful significance. Throughout the novel, "beauty" and "glory" are operative terms that allow Rodrigues to remain religious in the face of the seemingly meaningless pain among the Japanese peasants that he is forced to witness; however, at the climactic moment, Rodrigues's trial is this: is he willing to give up even religion, even his confession and love for the beautiful Christ, in order to save the lives of the innocent?

Christians versed in scriptural imagery are almost certain to see in Rodrigues's gesture a kind of kenosis or self-emptying move, perhaps even of the same sort that Paul describes in relation to the incarnation and death of Christ in his famed Phillipians hymn: "Let the same mind be in you that was in Christ Jesus, who, though he was in the form of God, did not regard equality with God as something to be exploited, but emptied himself, taking the form of a slave, being born in human likeness. And being found in human form, he humbled himself and became obedient to the point of death—even death on a cross" (Phil 2:5–8). When the slick, socially rewarding Christ of *Saved!'s* American Eagle Christian High fails, or even the more venerable "beautiful" Christ of *Silence* both fail, then what is left is the Christ found in the ugliness of self-emptying—but a self-emptying that gives life rather than denigrating it.

We have seen in this chapter that theology of the cross seeks to be theo-logos in the deepest sense: interrogating our own God-talk and that of the institutions that we create (including the church) in order to ask whether it is adequate to represent the scandal of a God who chooses to be found in the brokenness of Jesus of Nazareth precisely so that new possibilities for understanding God's action in the world might be discerned.

Questions

1. Do you find the notion that God suffers to be theologically helpful or not? Is it comforting, or not?
2. Would you agree with Bonhoeffer and Hall that a church of the cross is called to be at the margins and not the center of society?
3. Have you undergone moments of rupture in your own life that have fundamentally changed how you understand the nature of the divine/ultimate meaning in life? What changed, and why?
4. Can you agree with the idea (suggested by Endo's novel) that one might have to empty oneself even to the point of giving up one's religion in order to help the suffering? What might this look like today?

Suggestions for further reading

For an excellent recent summary of the role of the cross in Bonhoeffer's thought, see H. Gaylon Barker, *The Cross of Reality: Luther's Theologia Crucis and Bonhoeffer's Christology* (Minneapolis: Fortress, 2015). For primary texts that serve as good entry points into the work of the theologians mentioned in this chapter, see Douglas John Hall, *The Cross in Our Context: Jesus and the Suffering World* (Minneapolis: Fortress, 2003); Jürgen Moltmann, *The Crucified God: The Cross of Christ as the Foundation and Criticism of Christian Theology*, trans. R.A. Wilson and John Bowden

(Minneapolis: Fortress, 1993), and Eberhard Jüngel, *God as the Mystery of the World: On the Foundation of the Theology of the Crucified One in the Dispute Between Theism and Atheism*, trans. Darrell L. Guder (London: Bloomsbury T. & T. Clark; Reprint edition 2014). For a good range of articles on the question of whether God suffers or not, see T. J. White and J. Keating (eds.), *Divine Impassibility and the Mystery of Human Suffering* (Grand Rapids: Eerdmans, 2009). For a powerful theological application of themes from Moltmann especially, see Alan Lewis, *Between Cross and Resurrection: A Theology of Holy Saturday* (Grand Rapids: Eerdmans, 2001). For a text contexualizing Endo's novels within the broader sweep of Japanese thinking about the cross and theology, see Arata Miyamoto, *Embodied Cross: Intercontextual Reading of Theologia Crucis* (Eugene, OR: Wipf and Stock, 2010).

3

GLORY AND REALITY

What, then is the cross of Jesus? What does it mean? What does it disclose? What does it symbolize? What reality does it represent? The cross is the suffering of Jesus of Nazareth and it is the suffering of humanity. The cross means human beings rejecting human beings. It is human beings abandoning human beings. It shows how human beings, in the grip of demonic powers, are inflicting injustice on each other, tearing each other apart, destroying each other. The cross is the plot of organized religion blinded by its own power and orthodoxy and unable to tolerate those deeply and sincerely religious persons eager to restore faith in the God of love and mercy. And the cross discloses the complicity of socio-political powers ready to defend their self-interest at any cost, even at the expense of the law, even at the cost of the lives of those God-inspired persons faithful to the truth and devoted to love for others.[1]

1. Song, *Jesus, the Crucified People*, 99.

The Taiwanese theologian C. S. Song's words—taken from his provocatively titled text *Jesus, the Crucified People*—are emblematic of the fact that, as discussed in the last chapter, theologians interested in *theologia crucis* understand the critical edge of theology to apply, not only to conceptions of God and God's attributes, but to the political and social arrangements underpinned by these theological ideas. As we have been discussing, a key tenet of the theology of the cross is that *theology matters*—matters not only for personal piety and religious practice, but matters too for politics, psychology, sociology, and human interaction.

Thus, theology of the cross has, within the last several decades, proven itself to be a potent weapon in the hands of those who seek to subvert theologies that support unjust status quos, and to replace them with alternatives that are more faithful to the gospel by being more attuned to the power of that gospel to subvert human domination of the poor and of the earth. As we saw in the first chapter, this dual attack upon bad theology and bad politics was at the heart of Luther's own *theologia crucis*, and it is the aspect of his legacy that has endured and grown most significantly in our own day.

This chapter will examine some of those attempts in order to get at the question: what difference does the cross, and the God-conceptions that it discloses, make to the work of justice?

THE CROSS: GOD'S WORK OR HUMANITY'S?

One of the most significant aspects of contemporary theology (beginning in the late twentieth century) has been the fragmentation of theological discourse that comes about when an assumed authoritative center is shown to be simply one option among many. For many years in the West, the main voice of theology—despite its doctrinal diversity—was one of privilege: white, male, heterosexual, educated, and located in positions of cultural and ecclesial power. However, as the twentieth century continued, globalization became a factor in theology and church life; meanwhile, epoch-making struggles such as feminism and the civil rights movement progressed in the United States and Europe. The effect of this upon theology was to bring to the fore previously suppressed voices: those of women, African Americans, theologians from the "two-thirds world," LGBT Christians, and others who now had platforms (within the theological academy and the church) from which to contextualize the theological discourse previously dominated by such luminaries as Karl Barth, Paul Tillich, Karl Rahner, and others—contextualize it to speak to situations not previously comprehended by white Euro-American males.

Indeed, the liberation theology that emerged particularly from Latin American contexts in the mid-twentieth century had an ambiguous relationship to the retrieval of theology of the cross characteristic of Bonhoeffer, Moltmann, etc. On the one hand, the recovery of the centrality of the broken and crucified Jesus as a critical principal against theological/political domination was helpful. On the other hand, liberation theology was quick to remind its relatively affluent Western counterparts that what was at stake in *theologia crucis* is not simply existential questions of human meaning, but real questions of human bodies and their material circumstances. Jon Sobrino, a Jesuit priest who spent most of his ministry in El Salvador, makes the point sharply:

> [In Latin American theology] the "death of God" is viewed through the death of a human being. That death is real and widespread. If the death of God is the expression of a crisis in meaning,

> human death is the expression of a crisis in reality. It is not an experience of being orphaned or of a world that has come of age [Bonhoeffer] or of a Good Friday of the speculative mind [Hegel], but a real experience of the death of the poor, the oppressed, the Indian, the peasant. In Latin America, death does not simply mean the disappearance of that which had supposedly given meaning to things (in this case, God), but the triumph of injustice and sin. The theologically correct statement that sin caused the death of the Son is brought home to people in Latin America through the experience of sin continuing to cause the death of sons and daughters.[2]

In other words, if the tendency of Western theologians of the cross is to focus too much on the crucified God as a problem of academic theology, the burden of liberation theology is to use the cross of Christ as a lens through which to view the ongoing crucifixion of the poor and broken in the world.

IS GOD THE PROBLEM TO BE SOLVED?

Within the United States, feminist theology's opening salvo was Valerie Saiving's 1960 essay, "The Human Situation: A Feminine View," in which she argued that the retrieval of classical notions of sin by such prominent theologians as Paul Tillich and Reinhold Niebuhr emphasized that sinfulness is mainly tied to pride and human self-assertion.[3] Saiving's argument was that tying sin to pride (and thus, by extension, tying proper theology to humility) reflected a significant blind spot: pride, under the conditions of

2. Sobrino, *True Church and the Poor*, 32.

3. A reprint of this essay may be found in Christ, *WomanSpirit Rising*, 25–42.

patriarchy, is a distinctively male sin. To say that women have the same sort of sinfulness as males when sexism and global oppression of females is rampant is to misconstrue both theology and the world. Instead, argues Saiving (and she was soon supported by a number of feminist theological colleagues), the root sin to which females are tempted under the conditions of patriarchy is self-abnegation: allowing oneself and one's potential as a beloved creation of God to be stymied and whither under the burdens of patriarchal injustice. Under the conditions of patriarchy in which males on the whole have more power than females, "male" sin tends to be too much pride and self-assertion; meanwhile, "female" sin tends to be too much humility and self-neglect.

The impact of this line of argument upon theologizing about the cross became clear when feminist theology soon coalesced around critiques of traditional notions of the cross's role in atonement—reconciling humanity to God. While the Christian church has never held to one specific model of atonement, in both medieval theology and the Christian popular imagination the notion that Christ dies on the cross either as a substitute bearing the punishment that rightfully belonged to humanity (a view known as "substitutionary atonement" and associated with such key figures as Anselm of Canterbury[4]) or, relatedly, as a voluntary and innocent target of God's wrath towards human sin (an emphasis within the Reformation, including within Luther's theology) has certainly been popular within Christian preaching and teaching. Regardless of how the different modes of substitutionary atonement were nuanced, the structure was similar: human sin—tied often to the prideful assertion of human independence from God, as in the

4. Cf. Anselm, "Why God Became Man," 260–356.

common Christian reading of Genesis 3—merited God's wrath[5]; however, Christ the innocent victim follows God's plan and substitutes himself (or, as Acts 2:23 puts it, is "delivered up according to the definite plan and foreknowledge of God") as the bearer of God's punishment on the cross. Put provocatively: according to substitutionary atonement, human pride is the problem, but so too is God—God's wrath becomes a problem for atonement to solve.

The critique leveled against this account of atonement by feminist theology and other currents of liberation theology identifies a number of concerns. One, the notion that the cross is necessary to expunge God's wrath against human sin exemplifies the sort of blind spots that Saiving points out: assuming that the sins to which those with power are tempted (pride) is a universal sin rather than one conditioned by sociopolitical realities on the ground. Relatedly, this image of God as requiring the sacrifice of God's son to appease wrath appears problematic to the point that some feminist theologians have leveled the charge of "divine child abuse!" Indeed, Rita Nakashima Brock and Rebecca Ann Parker's influential text *Proverbs of Ashes: Violence, Redemptive Suffering, and the Search for What Saves Us* advanced the argument that too often glorification of the cross of Christ has had the effect of encouraging women especially to endure unjust suffering in the name of piety.[6]

Indeed, so often within Christian practice, Jesus' admonition to his followers to "take up the cross" (Matt 16:24), combined with valorization of Jesus' own humble submission to God's will on the cross, has lent itself to women especially being told that, for instance, putting up with an abusive husband is her "cross to bear." While a key principle of Christian theology generally is that "abuse does

5. Cf. Saler, "Transformation of Reason."

6. Brock and Parker, *Proverbs of Ashes.*

not invalidate right use," in this case feminist theologians (and others) have argued that the connections between substitutionary atonement and abusive social arrangements are too direct for substitutionary atonement to be salvageable. Indeed, we might say that their argument is that such critiques turn the theology of cross into a theology of glory precisely in Luther's sense: a misconstrual of God that supports an unjust status quo, in this case patriarchy and violence.

But if the event of the cross is not seen as an assuaging of God's wrath, if this view is rejected for both theological and ethical reasons, then what becomes of the theology of the cross?

THE DEATH OF THE TRUTHTELLER

In arguing for the possibility of rapprochement between a feminist sensibility sensitive to these concerns and Luther's *theologia crucis*, Deanna Thompson argues that

> where Luther and feminist theologians stand most closely together is in their reforming *sensibility* that gets worked out through shared methodological commitments. Both Luther and feminists are allied in their stinging critiques of dominant traditions. Both are well practiced in leveling a "No!" against the theologies of glory rampant in their context.[7]

According to many feminist and liberation theologians, the cross does not have to be seen as a kind of assuaging of divine wrath or act of divine violence in order to be a testimony to God's deep involvement with pain and

7. Thompson, "Becoming a Feminist Theologian," 81.

suffering. In fact, to assume that Jesus' death is in response to God's initiative is, on this account, to miss the point.

If, as we have been saying, the theology of the cross "calls the thing what it is" even as the principalities and powers of the world have a vested interest in keeping the world—and the church!—ideologically blinded, then it is natural to assume that those same powers will do all they can to suppress the word of truth from being spoken. Indeed, as in the case of the crucifixion of Jesus, once again it may be that the church and the *imperium* work together on this deception and repression. As ethicist Mark Lewis Taylor writes in his extensive study of how the criminal justice system in the United States mimics the injustices of Jesus' crucifixion,

> Jesus died, then, not only as a rebel in an imperial and politicized context. He also died as a blasphemer in the eyes of the religious establishment. The way of the executed God entails being not only on the underside of the many systems of imperial power but also on the downside of established religious leaders and their networks of power.[8]

To be a speaker of God's truth is to face the same opposition as the prophets in the Bible's day and our own. It is to face resistance, perhaps even resistance unto death.

On this view, the crucifixion of Jesus Christ is not viewed as a kind of satisfaction of God the Father vis-à-vis human sin; nor is it viewed as the cosmic mechanism of atonement without which forgiveness cannot take place. Instead, the crucifixion of Jesus Christ is seen as the outcome of the clash between God's mission of life (with all the truth-telling and opposition to injustice that that mission

8. Taylor, *Executed God*, 37.

entails, as depicted in the gospel narratives) and the forces of death and injustice in our world.

This, too, is in line with the human experience that God takes on in the incarnation.[9] When we look at our world, we see that those who confront the forces of systematic oppression in the world are often struck down by those forces—Gandhi, Martin Luther King Jr., Oscar Romero. If one lives, however imperfectly, on the side of the good, then one is likely to be treated as Jesus was. And the same is true for the church community that pledges, in the name of the crucified Messiah, to commit itself to the struggle for justice. As womanist (African-American feminist) scholar JoAnne Marie Terrell writes,

> As Jesus was innocent, when the community responds to the call to holiness, highlighting its members' innocence, it exposes the egregious nature of the crimes against them and against God, in Christ, and confirms the ultimacy of their liberatory claims. Thus . . . the cross is not taken up apart from what the rest of the story affirms; namely, that Jesus was God *incarnate*, who lived, struggled, and died in suffering solidarity with society's victims.[10]

But where there is cross, there is resurrection. A powerful political cartoon that circulated after the assassination of Dr. King shows Gandhi greeting him in the afterlife by saying, "The funny thing about assassins, Dr. King, is that they think they have killed you." Just as God is present in the Christ who is executed by the confluence of bad politics and bad religion that is so apparent in our own time, the

9. For a wonderfully nuanced theological account of this, cf. Kathryn Tanner, *Christ the Key*.

10. Terrell, "Our Mother's Gardens," 42; cf. also her *Power in the Blood? The Cross in the African American Experience*.

God who resurrected Jesus Christ from the dead does not abandon the work of justice once the forces of death have won their temporary victories. The theology of the cross is a theology of resistance to death in both the penultimate sense (the cross calls us to fight the forces of death and injustice on behalf of victims) and the ultimate sense (death does not have the last word, even in the case of the victims).

WHERE IS THE CROSS TODAY?

In his book *The Cross and the Lynching Tree*, African-American theologian James Cone quotes the following poem from Countee Cullen:

> The South is crucifying Christ again
> By all the laws of ancient rote and rule;
> The ribald cries of "Save Yourself" and "Fool"
> Din in his ears, the thorns grope for his brain . . .

The poem goes on to draw explicit connections between the crucifixion of Christ and the then-prevalent (Cullen's poem was written in 1922) open lynching of black men in the South. As Cone writes,

> Like Countee Cullen, many black poets, novelists, painters, dramatists, and other artists saw clearly what white theologians and clergy ignored and what black religious scholars and ministers merely alluded to: that in the United States, the clearest image of the Crucified Christ was the figure of an innocent black victim, dangling from the lynching tree.[11]

11. Cone, *Cross and the Lynching Tree*, 93.

While we might point to how much things have changed around race relations since 1922, an honest appraisal of the situation in the United States shows that the structures of white supremacy are still firmly in place, particularly in communities where militarized policing tactics continue to claim the lives of unarmed black suspects (as in the cases of Sandra Bland, Trayvon Martin, Michael Brown, and so many others). While it is the case that many religious leaders have been on the front lines of protest against these injustices,[12] we must also honestly say—with Bonhoeffer and Moltmann and Song, as well as so many others—that religion has just as often been the problem. The Klu Klux Klan will burn crosses on lawns and wear them on their uniforms, just as the marauding Christian crusaders of the past painted crosses on their shields as they carried out corrupt and horrific warfare against perceived enemies. No religious symbol is immune from being coopted into injustice, including the cross.

Far from denying this, *theologia crucis* provides a lens for acknowledging and intensifying the claim: part of the pathos of the cross is that it is equally employable as an instrument of oppression and an instrument of liberation. Moreover, there is no advance safeguard, no safety net of assurance that any given theological instance of discourse about the cross will be free from the potential to harm.

This means, among other things, that theology of the cross needs to strike a balance between the need to call out misuse of power and the need to be continually self-suspicious; it is the "speech/stammering" dialectic mentioned in the introduction. Theology of the cross can give rise to prophetic speech on behalf of justice; at the same time, anyone seeking to carry out such speech needs to be realistic about the ongoing potential of even the most defensible claims

12. Cf. Francis, *Ferguson and Faith*.

(theological, political, or otherwise) to become ideological and oppressive when wielded without nuance or sensitivity to context. This self-suspicion, too, can be carried out in the name of the cross. To put it bluntly: absolute theological certainty must be one of the things that we allow the cross of Christ to crucify in us. Just as the cross permits us to be broken, imperfect people, it also calls us to recognize our status as broken, imperfect theologians.

But despite these ever-present dangers, those seeking to "call things what they are" in our own world have found in the cross of Christ a powerful theological symbol for naming the effects of evil and death in our world as well as the presence of God in the deepest depths of suffering. For instance, Kittredge Cherry and Douglas Blanchard's *The Passion of Christ: A Gay Vision* adapts the classical stations of the cross (in which the faithful are invited, via art, to follow in the footsteps of Jesus during his passion ordeal and crucifixion) in order to depict the loneliness and trials of contemporary urban gay men as they face homophobia and violence in the modern city.[13] Cone, referenced above, sees in the cross God's unrelenting partiality for those who are marginalized and oppressed, as Jesus himself was. Theologians who work in and alongside "crucified people" (Song) have found in the cross a powerful symbol, but a symbol that does not depart from history (as in the common opposition between "symbolic" and "literal") but rather drives theology deeper *into* history itself. Symbol, in this case, illuminates reality, and does so in ways that discomfort and disrupt our normal lenses upon the world. But this, too, is salutary (and perhaps even salvific) for both theology and the Christian life.

What are we to make of all this? In a provocative and beautiful statement about the relationship of the four

13. Cherry and Blanchard, *Passion of Christ: A Gay Vision.*

canonical Gospel narratives (Matthew, Mark, Luke, and John) to God's ongoing presence and saving work in the world, Vítor Westhelle posits that "the canon, in preserving the apostolic witness, functions as a sort of template for a gospel that continues to be told in old and new stories, in parables that are still being crafted for every people in their own context."[14] If we accept this as a principle, then we might say that the crucifixion and resurrection of Jesus, in addition to being a historical event of crucial (and to a certain extent irreplaceable) significance, is also a kind of template for recognizing God's ongoing way of interacting with the world. As we will discuss in the next chapter, the cross gives us eyes to see how God continues to be present in that which the world rejects, and gives us a theological vocabulary both for naming that presence and allowing it to galvanize us for action.

Questions

1. Can you think of instances in which a particular theological notion either supports or subverts injustice? Under what circumstances can theology help the work of justice, and when does it hurt?
2. Do you think that it is crucial to understand the cross as God's punishment, or does the notion that it was solely a human act against God's intention make more sense to you?
3. What are some of the most intriguing artistic and literary depictions of the cross of which you are aware? Movies, books, art, etc.?

14. Westhelle, *After Heresy*, 162.

Suggestions for further reading

For a useful collection of essays assessing the viability of the theology of cross for the project of liberation of humanity and creation, see Marit Treltstad (ed.), *Cross Examinations: Readings on the Meaning of the Cross Today* (Minneapolis: Augsburg, 2006). James Cone's powerful meditation on the relationship between the cross of Christ and the lynching of black people in the United States can be found in his *The Cross and the Lynching Tree* (Maryknoll, NY: Orbis, 2013); similarly, see JoAnne Marie Terrell, *Power in the Blood? The Cross in the African American Experience* (Eugene, OR: Wipf and Stock, 2005). For more on the cross and Latin American liberation theology, see Vítor Westhelle, *The Scandalous God: The Use and Abuse of the Cross* (Minneapolis: Fortress, 2007).

4

THE COMMUNITY OF FIDELITY TO THE CRUCIFIED

As we have seen in the chapters above, theology of the cross impacts both one's conception of God and one's ethics towards those who are marginalized in the world. This certainly has implications for individual Christians; however, in this final chapter, we will widen the scope and ask about the churches that take faithfulness to the gospel—and discipleship to Jesus Christ—as their reason for being. What does *theologia crucis* look like for the community of Christ's life in the world?

FIDELITY TO THE CRUCIFIED

As we saw in the first chapter, Luther's own view of the church reflected his emphasis on the cross. Strikingly, since the nature of the true church was at issue in the Reformation from the beginning, Luther intentionally incorporated "cross" into his ecclesiology as a shorthand, not only for suffering, but for the church truly perceiving itself as God's work. As Vítor Westhelle explains,

> When Luther wrote On the Councils and the Church (1538) he listed 7 marks of the church, among others that apply to standards of sanctification . . . [In Luther's list] there is a further external sign, which had not appeared explicitly before neither in his nor in Melachthon's writings about the church: cross and suffering. This seventh sign reveals the church as this community that, even when confessed to be one and holy, still lives under the sign of the cross, in transience, in trial, in weakness, in infamy, in vulnerability, in doubt and even forsakenness, attesting that in these realities, as in the Cross of Christ itself, there is God.[1]

Because, as becomes clear particularly in his lectures on the book of Genesis, Luther understood the true church to be an hidden under the realities of weakness (as opposed to lust for earthly power and domination) and persecution for holding steadfast to the gospel, he could only see one path forward for real believers: undergoing the same sort of suffering that characterized Christ's own fidelity to God's promises in the face of opposition. For Luther, no less than for the early church, to be a Christian thus necessitated the possibility of martyrdom, and this reality (both conceptually and historically) informs his *theologia crucis*.

In fact, in the Genesis lectures, Luther uses this theme to draw a contrast that is operative throughout his theology: the idea that the true church is, throughout history, a minority and indeed often invisible assembly (the church

1. Westhelle, "Communio," para. 8. Cf. also his *Church Event*.

of Abel) that is placed within the milieu of the larger, more worldly successful church of Cain. "Moreover, here the church begins to be divided into two churches: the one which is the church in name but in reality is nothing but a hypocritical and bloodthirsty church; and the other one, which is without influence, forsaken, and exposed to suffering and the cross, and in the sight of that hypocritical church is truly Abel, that is, vanity and nothing."[2] This allows Luther to establish a key point about the church that was crucial for the Reformation: in an era in continuity with the prior Christian suspicion of novelty and innovation, Luther tracing the "true church" of Cain and Abel into his own day allowed him to argue that it was the medieval church's embrace of such innovations as veneration of saints, purgatory, the papacy, and other structures synonymous with "theology of glory" that in fact left the medieval church guilty of innovation. This argument would become influential as the Reformation spread.[3]

Douglas John Hall, whom we discussed in Chapter 2 above, has emphasized this ecclesial dimension by arguing consistently that Luther's theology of the cross should serve as a resource for churches in European and North American contexts who face the end of *de facto* Christendom and full cultural disestablishment; if Luther's ecclesiology of the cross suggests that the true church will always be somewhat at the margins of what the world calls powerful, then churches should embrace the cross as a bulwark against false prosperity.[4] As various contexts in North America and elsewhere continue to see the rise of "prosperity gospel" and other success-oriented theological movements, it remains

2. Luther, "Genesis Lectures,"in *Luther's Works*, 1:252.

3. Cf. Saler, *Between Magisterium and Marketplace*.

4. Cf. Hall, *Waiting for Gospel: An Appeal* and *Cross in Our Context*.

to be seen the extent to which ecclesiologies drawn from a cross-centered perspective can gain and retain traction on the ecclesial landscape.

WHAT IT LOOKS LIKE WHEN IT GOES RIGHT

In 1996, a group of terrorists in Algeria announced to the world that they had killed seven French Trappist monks whom they had kidnapped from the monastery of Tibherine there; the monks had been held hostage for two months prior. Father Christian de Chergé, one of the monks that was killed, left behind this last testament that his family found after his death. It includes the following words:

> My death, clearly, will appear to justify those who hastily judged me naive or idealistic: "Let him tell us now what he thinks of it!" But these people must realize that my most avid curiosity will then be satisfied. This is what I shall be able to do, if God wills—immerse my gaze in that of the Father, to contemplate with him his children of Islam just as he sees them, all shining with the glory of Christ, the fruit of his Passion, filled with the Gift of the Spirit, whose secret joy will always be to establish communion and to refashion the likeness, delighting in the differences.
>
> For this life given up, totally mine and totally theirs, I thank God who seems to have wished it entirely for the sake of that joy in everything and in spite of everything. In this "thank you," which is said for everything in my life from now on, I certainly include you, friends of yesterday and today, and you my friends of this place, along with my mother and father, my brothers and sisters and their families—the hundredfold granted as was promised!

> And you also, the friend of my final moment, who would not be aware of what you were doing. Yes, for you also I wish this "thank you"—and this *adieu*—to commend you to the God whose face I see in yours.
>
> And may we find each other, happy "good thieves," in Paradise, if it pleases God, the Father of us both. Amen.[5]

Such is a life lived within the optics of the cross—including eyes to see purported enemies as "the fruit of Jesus' Passion." But what must go into producing such a life? Where does the theology of the cross fit into it?

I should say that, as implied by my framing the question this way, I regard Fr. de Chergé's statement as a near-perfect instance of how the Christian worldview, in genuinely incarnational rhetorical fashion (as Eric Auerbach noticed decades ago), blends the most eschatologically sublime understanding of the beautified vision characteristic of Christian hopes for with an earthy, humane awareness of human fallibility and epistemological humility. In other words, it exemplifies *theologia crucis*.

I propose that, if we are to understand the church as a community of fidelity to the one crucified for love of the world, then we should draw that picture within the parameters of the following two insights from the example, not only the of Tibherine monks, but of the tradition stemming from Luther and encapsulated in the literature on the cross that we have been discussing in this book.

1. God's people are called to love the world precisely *as* the world to a greater degree than the world loves itself.

5. This translation by the Monks of Mount Saint Bernard Abbey in Leicester, England can be found at http://www.firstthings.com/article/1996/08/006-last-testament. See also Salenson, *Christian de Chergé*.

2. Cultivating such love, paradoxically but inexorably, requires deep immersion in the particular gifts of the church—the word preached, the body and blood received, ongoing and rigorous catechesis in theology (both doctrinal and speculative), art, aesthetics, spiritual disciplines, and so on.

In other words, I'm suggesting that the example of the brothers of Tibherine, precisely in its glorious strangeness, shows us that it is precisely the act of going more deeply into the gifts of the church in a manner that is formative of a different kind of subjectivity that allows the church to be incarnationally engaged in the world.

In order to demonstrate this, we will return in this last section to Luther, this time to a different writing: his *Freedom of a Christian*.

THE HORIZON OF NEED AND THE THICKNESS OF THE CHRISTIAN LIFE

The argument of Luther's famed 1520 treatise *On the Freedom of a Christian* has at its core a thesis that Luther knew would be counterintuitive both by the synergistic soteriological standards of his day and, more penetratingly, by the standards of what Luther took to be the epistemological "default setting" of the Old Adam when it considers the role of human effort both in salvation and in worldly ethics. Simply put, Luther's target is the notion that only a synergistic model of salvation—one in which human agency responds to God's initial donation of grace by doing those good works which are within them (*facere quod in se est*) to the benefit, not only of their own standing vis-à-vis God's judgment, but also to the neighbor—can produce ethical action. Pious doubt about one's salvation, so the argument goes, translates to pious action manifested most naturally in works of charity on behalf of one's neighbor. The parallels to calls for a soteriology that replaces monergistic assurance with synergistic risk contingent on human agency in service to ethical care for the earth are fairly direct in this case.

What was behind Luther's rejection of this soteriology? At stake was not simply Luther's theological breakthrough vis-à-vis justification of the individual by grace through faith apart from works, but also his ethics. For Luther, far from it being the case that one needs a cooperative model of salvation in order to give sufficient theological grounding and impetus for charitable works on behalf of the neighbor, the exact opposite is in fact the case: *only* under conditions of justification by grace through faith apart from works (that is, only under conditions whereby we do not *need* to do good works for our neighbor to be justified by God) are we free to do good works that are truly *for* the neighbor and not for ourselves.

The logic is this: if I must somehow do good works—however praiseworthy and even necessary for the neighbor's well-being—in order to merit justification, then those works are inescapably bound up in an economy of merit and reward that is not only existentially intolerable (how can I possibly know when I have done enough, and how can I possibly remain in any sort of pious doubt about that when the stakes are so high?) but also fully lacking in genuine *caritas*. The motive of care in such cases can never purely be the desired good of the neighbor. The horizon of need being addressed is not the neighbor's, but mine; or, at least, when push comes to shove, if the two horizons contradict each other at all, mine has to win out over the neighbor's. The high school senior who realizes that she needs more "community service" lines of her college application and thus walks down to the soup kitchen may well do some proximate good for the homeless there, but the dominant horizon of need is hers and not the suffering neighbors ostensibly being served.

However, to the extent that the Word is received that we are justified by grace through faith entirely apart from our own works, then the soteriological and ethical framework is secured by which the horizon of the neighbor's need can take precedence over my own and thus shape the framework of the ethical response. As Luther puts it, the Christian

> needs none of these things for his righteousness and salvation. Therefore he should be guided in all his works by this thought and contemplate this one thing alone, that he may serve and benefit others in all that he does, considering nothing except the need and the advantage of his neighbor. Accordingly the Apostle commands us to work with our hands so that we may give to the needy, although he might have said that we should work to support ourselves. He says, however, "that he may be able to give to those in need" [Eph. 4:28]. This is what makes caring for the body a Christian work, that through its health and comfort we may be able to work, to acquire, and lay by funds with which to aid those who are in need, that in this way the strong member may serve the weaker, and we may be sons of God, each caring for and working for the other, bearing one another's burdens and so fulfilling the law of Christ [Gal. 6:2]. This is a truly Christian life. Here faith is truly active through love [Gal 5:6], that is, it finds expression in works of the freest service, cheerfully and lovingly done, with which a man willingly serves another without hope of reward; and for

> himself is satisfied with the fullness and wealth of his faith.[6]

When we are freed of the existential burden of a soteriology that requires our good works for righteousness, we are entered into a more kenotic ethical economy whereby the horizon of the neighbor's need overtakes the need for us to preserve our own righteousness. It is liberating to do something purely for its own delight and goodness rather than because one expects to gain something by it. What's more, when our focus is reoriented away from our own need and toward the horizon of the neighbor, that which we do inevitably becomes more helpful and more just simply by the changed motivation and "economy" of activity.

So what emerges here, to repeat, is a situation in which, perhaps to a scandalous degree, Luther is understanding the public vocation of the Christian (and, by extension, the church) as kenotically emptying out its own "Old Adam" perceptions of how to be theologically righteous (i.e., sufficiently pure, religious, "churchy," etc.) in order to address the horizon of need of the neighbor—with all the messiness, "secularity," and gritty immersion into the blood, sweat, and tears of our world that that implies. If we do not "have" to work, then our work does not "have" to take on any prefabricated "religious" shape. It can take the shape that it needs to take in order to truly be work done for the neighbor. We can relinquish "religious" control. Such a kenotic engagement *is* the work of the Spirit in our world, and ecclesiology should take its cue from that.

Within *On the Freedom of a Christian*, it is clear—the *only* way that the sinful Christian can be freed to engage the neighbor within the messy horizon of the neighbor's need (think of the Algerian monks giving medical care to Muslim

6. Luther, *On the Freedom of a Christian*, in *Luther's Works*, 31:365.

villagers as other Muslims threaten to kill them) is for the Christian to engage in substantive, ritualized, and ongoing immersion into the thickness of the church's own unique practices—again, hearing the gospel that we are freed from the demands of law and the demands of self-justification, receiving God's own self at the Eucharist, and—and here is the challenge to Lutherans where proper distinction between law and gospel is at the heart of Lutheran theological identity—ongoing spiritual formation that allows for Christians to have this gospel counteract the formation that we receive elsewhere.

THE OPTICS OF THE MARKET AND OF THE CROSS

If that is true, then what exactly needs to be counteracted?

When I was a parish pastor in a heavily churched area of an inner city, I once received a phone call from a local newspaper asking me if our congregation wanted to place an ad in the paper's "Religion Classifieds" section (which already tells you something right there). Without my asking, he proceeded to tell me that many local churches found it helpful to get the word out about their service times, etc.

This is common practice, and I have no real problems with it. But then he proceeded to say the following, "After all, it never hurts to get a leg up on the competition."

Think of that imagery. Churches advertising so as to get a leg up on their "competition" (i.e., other Christian churches). Trinity Lutheran vs. Christ the King Lutheran, advertising their wares in a manner structurally indistinguishable from Wal-Mart vs. Target.

My point is not to knock church advertising. My point is that I suspect many of us American Christians have internalized, wittingly or not, the notion that the church operates in what sociologists have called a "spiritual marketplace" in which our functional role is to provide a "product" in order to meet a given "demand." I would argue that the main issue with missional theology in the mainline churches has to do with a "if we build it, they will come" mentality; thus, what we should notice here is how neatly that mentality corresponds with capitulation to consumerism.

That's one problem. But it's a problem that we are not going to get our heads around until we realize how thoroughly consumerism comes with its own theology, its own psychology, its own ideas around what truth, beauty, and meaning constitute.

The average American views hundreds, if not thousands, of advertisements every day (between Internet, television, t-shirts, magazines, etc.). What is the goal of such advertising? The main goal of advertising is to poke a tiny hole in our lives, a hole that can then be filled by the product on sale. If you put these two facts together, then the psychological picture that emerges is one in which most of us are walking around having thousands of tiny holes poked into our self-image, our sense of happiness, every day.

And the effects of this are not benign. A stunning recent piece of art on the front of an avant-garde magazine focusing on women's issues puts it bluntly. The image is of a young woman in heavy makeup, shaded in such a way as to simultaneously imply overuse of cosmetics and perhaps even physical or mental abuse, looking down, and the caption simply reads: "Call Us Ugly to Sell Us Shit." The feeling of ugliness, the attack upon the peace that comes with one's worth coming from something other than work and consumption, translates into further consumption.

We know the concrete effects of this. Eating disorders rampant among women *and* men. Personal household debt is through the roof. The list could go on. But all of these material effects are tied up in the deeper material problem, and that is this: *we cannot be satisfied.* And what I mean by that is not that we personally are incapable of being satisfied, but rather that we are all caught in a matrix of forces that have a deep interest in ensuring that we *will* not be satisfied, because satisfaction is dangerous.

The word "satisfaction" comes from the Latin *satis facere*, and it literally means to "make enough," that is, to be in a condition in which one feels that one has enough. In the twenty-first century we North Americans, along with an increasing percentage of the rest of the planet, are caught amidst forces who would be deeply threatened were we all to collectively decide that we are "satisfied," that we have enough of a given product. If I'm satisfied with my blue jeans, I'm threatening the sale of Levi's. If I'm satisfied with my car, I'm of concern to Toyota. Indeed, the main indicator by which we measure the health of national economies in geopolitical terms is the GDP, which measures *growth* of economies as the primary indication that they are healthy.

This is not to say that Toyota, Diesel, the government, or anyone else is evil, though, because *they too* are caught up in the system of having to sell in order to survive, in order for people to feed their families. This is not "us against them." This is us against ourselves. And that's a spiritual problem.

One way we might conceptualize this is to think of the "optics" of the market. How does consumerism teach us to "see" the world?

The theologian David Bentley Hart writes,

> The market transcends ideologies; it is the post-Christian culture of communication, commerce, and values characteristic of modernity, the myth by which the economies, politics, and mores of the modern are shaped, the ideal space where

> desire is fashioned; it is the place that is every place, the distance of all things, no longer even the market square, which is a space of meetings, a communal space, but simply the arid, empty distance that consumes every other distance.[7]

Hart credits this market "empty distance" as having enormous power to shape desire (and thus, by extension, desired ends); moreover, he envisions the market not as a rival public to the church but rather as the paradigmatic anti-public, a "no-space" that can thus insinuate itself into every space. Hart's account also proposes a link between the autonomous modern self who misconstrues freedom as pure autonomy to follow desire and the interested amenability of the marketplace to precisely such a formed personality. The hinge between the two is commodification, not simply of material products, but of those features of a person's identity (particularly those formed in communities outside the marketplace, e.g., religious faith) that are not immediately possessed of an exchange-value within the market. "The market, after all, which is the ground of the real in modernity, the ungrounded foundation where social reality occurs, makes room only for values that can be transvalued, that can be translated into the abstract valuations of univocal exchange."[8]

When the marketplace shapes our identity—when all of the holes that advertising pokes into our identities come home to roost—then the effects are devastating both for our own identities and our communities. Think again of that image of the woman: commodification is abuse, but it is also the same sort of erasure, of eff-face-ment, that comes with both overuse of cosmetics and the facelessness conferred by abuse. We live amidst powerful forces (beyond any

7. Hart, *Beauty of the Infinite*, 431.

8. Ibid., 432.

given individuals; think of the Bible's talk of "principalities and powers") are at work keeping people *deeply* (one might even say "spiritually") dissatisfied so that the systems that profit from such dissatisfaction may flourish.[9]

From the perspective of *theologia crucis*, what is an alternate worldview to the one shaped solely by the marketplace?

Let us return to the Heidelberg Disputation discussed in Chapter 1: a theologian of the cross calls a thing what it is. Why? For Luther, it is for this reason: on the cross, God takes the form of what is ugly. Jesus was a peasant carpenter and itinerant teacher from a backwater town who briefly engaged large crowds for a month or so, eventually fell out of their favor, and was crucified as a criminal by the Roman empire (one of the most shameful deaths for a Jew). God's truth in Christ took the form of what the world found ugly and pathetic.

This heritage from Luther—training us to see the presence of God in that which the world despises, calls ugly, regards as worthless—may be one of the most stunningly relevant aspects of our tradition in a world in which what Luther might call a "theology of glory" (that is, assuming that truth is most present in that which is beautiful, powerful, well-praised, etc.) dominates the logic of the marketplace. If the marketplace gives us a kind of optics, a "way of seeing" that sees ugliness in order to keep us purchasing, then the "optics" of the cross trains us instead to see the world as God's good creation in which it is precisely the outcasts, the marginalized, and the "ugly" in which we might expect to see God's Spirit most at work (note that this applies to people, but perhaps increasingly also to creation itself as it suffers the effects of our constant need to consume unsustainably).

9. Cf. Saler, *Between Magisterium and Marketplace*.

What does this have to say to the community that seeks to be faithful to the cross? I think it's this: if God hides in suffering, in that which the world calls weak, then perhaps one of the most significant contributions that Lutheran Christianity might bring to our context's ongoing conversations about "truth, beauty, meaning, and justice" might be to think with others—Christian or not—as to how our minds have been trained to see beauty in those places advantageous to the marketplace, and to ask then how a different kind of optics, a different kind of "eyes" for the world, might disclose the presence of truth in that which cannot be easily commodified and sold within what Hart calls the "agon" of the market. To the extent that we as a culture can gradually emerge from our addiction to the consumerism that is killing us, it will not only have material effects but also spiritual effects. And one of those spiritual effects is that the good news, the gospel of a God who hides in weakness and suffering in order to find us and the world that God loves precisely amidst that suffering, might become a story that resonates with the pathos of the world to an even greater extent. This is what I mean when I say that an incarnational logic of the cross, born from formation by the gospel and its gifts, results in a situation in which the properly formed theologian, the properly formed Christian, loves the world more than the world loves itself.

The community of fidelity to the cruficied—the church—cannot call the world ugly to sell it shit, or even to sell it gospel. The church must call the world blessed to preach gospel to it.

IMPLICATIONS

I've suggested that Luther's *On the Freedom of a Christian* teaches us that the gospel frees God's people to engage the horizon of the neighbor's need apart from the economies of self-justification. But I've also argued that this is not a one-off insight but requires ongoing and deep formation in the spiritual gifts and disciplines of the church. In incarnational fashion, the deeper we go into the things of Christ, the more "secular" (worldly) we become in that we engage more deeply the world qua world as the site of God's love and of God's redemption (this is what Bonhoeffer was getting at the end of this life, I'm convinced—his saying that the Christian life needs to become more fully worldly is not a departure from the quasi-monastic vision of *Life Together*, but the further extension and radicalizing of it.).

I've suggested that part of what is at stake (and in keeping with the optical themes of Fr. De Chergé's letter) is a kind of optics of the cross that resists the optics of the marketplace. But here again formation and spiritual discipline is key. It is not optional as to whether or not we are formed—whatever formation is not done by the church, the market will do for us. Rather than thinking of church formation as a bunkering down in a kind of alternative society, the fundamentally Lutheran theological insight is that going deeper into the particulars of the church and the thickness of Christian life is not a retreat from the world, but a deeper dive into it. As the church becomes more itself, it becomes more secular, because the *saeculum* belongs to God by creation and to Christ by redemption.

Questions

1. Based on the advertisements that you encounter in your day-to-day life, what do you feel that you are being taught to desire?
2. If you are a part of a faith community, what role does the cross play in the life of it? If not, how would you

describe the Christian faith communities of which you are aware in terms of the role that suffering, marginalization, poverty, etc. play in the life of those churches?

3. Do you agree that Christians are called to love the world more than it loves itself? Why or why not?

Suggestions for further reading

For an analysis of how theology and its truth claims interact with various "markets" in our age, see Robert C. Saler, *Between Magisterium and Marketplace: A Constructive Account of Theology and the Church* (Minneapolis: Fortress, 2014). For a theological inquiry into the nature of how desires are shaped, see James K. A. Smith, *Desiring the Kingdom: Worship, Worldview, and Cultural Formation* (Grand Rapids: Baker, 2009). For more on the work and martyrdom of the monks of the Tibhirine monastery in Algeria, see John W. Kiser, *The Monks of Tibhirine: Faith, Love, and Terror in Algeria* (New York: St. Martin's Griffin, 2002). For a powerful mediation on the church as a community of fidelity to the crucified, cf. Theodore W. Jennings, *Transforming Atonement: A Political Theology of the Cross* (Minneapolis: Fortress, 2009).

CONCLUSION

At the outset of our investigation, I suggested that the most useful guiding principle for navigating contemporary theologies of the cross is that *theologia crucis* provokes, within theology, an interplay of speech and "stuttering." Having reached the end of our brief tour of the multifaceted ways in which the cross of Jesus Christ factors in to the work of theologians who seek to be faithful both to the scandalous testimony of the crucified Messiah found in the gospel narratives and to the ongoing crucifixion of injustice's victory in our own time, what can we now say about the ways in which the cross both disrupts and empowers speech?

By way of conclusion, I would offer the following summary observations for your consideration:

1). *Theologia crucis from Luther's time to ours has had much variety, but also some key features in common.* As we have seen, each theologian who deals with the cross does so from her own context, and sometimes differences in context lead to different (or even competing) emphases in their view of the cross's importance. However, *theologia crucis* coalesces around a broadly shared understanding that the role of theology that is rooted in the cross is to unmask theological strategies that portray God as aligned with the dominant powers of the day ("glory") in order to deconstruct any perceived divine sanction for injustice. *Theologica crucis* is deconstructive; it is "combat theology" against God-images that support the status quo when the status quo is demonic.

2). *In our day, critique of "glory" is first and foremost theological idolatry critique.* Perhaps the most salient feature of Luther's distinction between theology of the cross and theologies of "glory" in our own time has to do with idolatry critique. But, as the various complexities within the theological literature that we have examined show, the task of discerning idolatrous theological formulations is not simply a matter of deciding, once and for all, that some forms of God-talk are perpetually okay and others are not.

For instance, it is easy for many theologians to say that the sort of easy "prosperity gospel" hawked by televangelists and internet gurus—promising material success to Christians who are sufficiently "faithful" in their piety, prayer lives, and personal donations—is bunk. Indeed, it is precisely the theology of the cross (which, as we have seen, understands the Christian life to be one of seeing God at work in the broken things of this world and joining God's work in solidarity there) that helps us to dismiss this line of thinking. However, just as the most powerful idols in our own lives are not the things that we generally know to be harmful (excessive eating, drug use, violent pornography, etc.) but rather the things which are good (family, security, patriotism, etc.), the most effective theological idols are not the statements which basic reflection might show to be false ("Those with enough faith can always be healed of cancer!"), but rather statements that in and of themselves might be true but are wielded in such a way as to promote injustice.

An example might be helpful. As I write these final pages, controversy is raging in the United States over the "Black Lives Matter" movement. The assertion that "black lives matter," leveraged successfully on social media and in national discussion, is a direct response to growing public awareness of egregious police brutality (often leading to death) towards unarmed black men and women. However, that strategy has faced opposition from those who want to insist in turn that "all lives matter." Now, taken in the abstract, "all lives matter" is of course a true statement. However, when the slogan "all lives matter" is used as a way of dismissing the very particular and pressing concerns raised by Black Lives Matter activists, then the true statement becomes ideological idolatry.

So it is even with *theologia crucis*. When a woman being abused by a loved one is told to "bear the cross" of her oppression in patience, then Jesus' warnings about the cross—that discipleship in a hostile world will involve suffering—has been removed from its context of truth and placed in service to a demonic ideology of patriarchy and abuse. However, when Christians fighting patriarchy appeal to solidarity with the "crucified" of the world (including battered women) and see this solidarity as them bearing the cross, then the same theological theme has been recast in a liberative, life-giving, and realistic direction.

There is no theological notion that is idolatry-proof. No true statement is immune to being used ideologically and harmfully. *Theologia crucis*, then, is one tool that theology and the church has to be on the critical watch for the ways in which idolatry and its death-dealing effects can take hold of even the most time-honored theological notions and twist them into tools of spiritual and material oppression.

3). *Theologia crucis in our time bears witness to a slow shift away from atonement models that see the cross as a consequence of God's wrath and towards models that see the cross as God's full and loving incarnation into the human experience.* Atonement models (such as substitutionary atonement) that see the cross as a necessary element of assuaging God's wrath towards humanity have never gone away, and likely never will. And indeed, they are compatible with some construals of *theologia crucis*—Luther himself tended to view atonement in those terms. However, as we have seen, in the centuries since the Reformation theology has seen a gradual shift away from the dominance of this sort of understanding. Increasingly, the cross is seen as humanity's resistance to Jesus' acts of love, mercy, and truth, particularly given that these acts brought him into opposition against the religious and political authorities of his day.

God's willingness to undergo the cross in Jesus is thus not only a sign of God's ongoing opposition to forces of death in our world, but it also shows the radicality of the incarnation: God takes on the entire human experience, even unto death. And God's resurrection of Christ signals that even death cannot defeat God's redemptive mission in the world.

Put simply, contemporary *theologia crucis* is more inclined to make sinful humanity the artisans of the cross, not God. God is not the problem to be solved; God is the architect of persisting love and unremitting redemption in the creation that God has made and in Christ has/is still redeeming.

So what is the future of the cross?

As we have seen, to speak theologically about the cross is to speak soberly about the places where God chooses to be found amidst the world's pain. Which means that, in order to anticipate the directions in which *theologia crucis* might go in the future, we might take as our orientation the question: what will be the direction of creation's pain in the future? About what will God's people be called to theologize, and in what spaces of marginalization will the community of fidelity to the crucified be found?

1). *Ecological Degradation*—as the effects of global climate change, water shortages, conflicts over oil, and other symptoms of environmental damage impact our world, theology in general is going to have to speak soberly yet hopefully about God's presence amidst the coming pain. To be sure, a number of excellent Christian theologians have, for decades, been theologizing well about Christian care for the environment.[1] However, further work needs to be done on how the critical principles of *theologia crucis* can serve to point out the ways in which numerous human ideologies—including theology—can either help or harm God's creation, and also the poorest human populations who are most vulnerable to the effects of degradation in our environment.

New Testament scholar Barbara Rossing has argued vigorously against the notion—popularized by such popular theological artifacts as the *Left Behind* series—that the image of God's salvation of the world present in the book of Revelation is violent; instead, she points out that it is the image of the crucified Lamb that signifies God's triumph over that which would oppress what God has made.[2] This direction, it seems to me, is promising for future work in thinking how that which human greed and selfishness is currently crucifying—that is, creation itself—might be defended on the basis of a theology that locates God within

1 For instance, see the excellent discussion by Cynthia Moe-Lobeda in *Resisting Structural Evil.*

2. Rossing, *Rapture Exposed*

the suffering of creation rather than in a position of "glory," that is, dominion and domination.

2). *Global focus*—as the vitality of the Christian church moves away from its historic Western centers (e.g., Europe and the United States) and continues to thrive in Africa, Asia, Latin America, etc., then all theology will need to continue to react to shifting contextual concerns. This impacts not only issues, but also worldview. For instance, a number of churches in African contexts have a more robust understanding of the world as a field of contest between various spirits (holy, demonic, and otherwise) than what many mainline churches in the United States and Europe might affirm. Given that, as I've argued, *theologia crucis* is a theology designed for combat with the "principalities and powers" of injustice and death wherever these are found, then how will the nature of theologizing about these demonic influences shift as Christian theology lives into a non-Euro-centric identity?

3. *Interfaith work*—On the one hand, as we have seen, the scandal of the cross in its full effect trades on particularly Christian affirmations about Jesus. For the cross to have its full effect, the Christian narrative understands God to be uniquely present in that event. As Christians, though, continue to live into realities of religious pluralism that Luther, for instance, never had to face, then how might commitments to respecting religious difference continue to shape our articulation of the significance of the cross?

4. *Theologia Crucis beyond the Church*—as we have seen, some of the sharpest deconstructive edges of *theologia crucis* have been aimed at Christian churches specifically. What might it mean for theologians to engage the ways in which themes and imagery congruent with the theology of the cross have escaped (or might escape) the confines of specifically church, or even Christian, discourse? This

would involve ongoing engagement with film, art, literature, video games, Internet memes, and all of the other ways in which contemporary conversations about truth, beauty, and meaning have moved beyond the church—even as the church, with its ongoing witness to Christ crucified and resurrected, may yet reclaim a life-giving place in those conversations if it is willing (ala Bonhoeffer) to follow God to the margins rather than insist on a privileged place at the center.

5. *The Cross and Life's Meaning*—much of our conversation has focused upon the social and political ramifications of the theology of the cross. It is worth noting here, though, that theology seeks also to address the deep existential questions of life's meaning. What is it that makes a life well-lived? How does the gospel provide meaning to life, not in a purely therapeutic sense, but in the deeper sense of orientation towards that which is true and good? And what does the cross have to do with this?

Recently, my seminary community was shocked by the death of a highly respected theologian who taught for us. His teaching and written work has been deeply influential upon a whole host of students. His death appears to have been by his own hand.

His last published article, a meditation on Christian theology and depression, reads now like a kind of harbinger of the death to come. He wrote as if he knew that his depression would overcome him. At the end of a life lived well, and lived seeking out the implications of the gospel of the crucified Christ, this Christian went to the foot of the cross as a broken man himself. On one (very real) level, it was and is a tragedy. However, speaking only for myself, I also see in my friend's death a startling depiction of the cross of the very Jesus in whom he believed. All of us will go to that cross, and we will go empty-handed, bearing no merits of our own. Even the greatest of us, even those greatest *at religion*, will find ourselves broken. Just as God had to bring life out of death in Christ's tomb, so too must God work within our own lives to make right what has been left for dead. "The ground at the foot of the cross is level," goes the old saying. But if the gospel carried in *theologia crucis* is true, then our broken selves and our dead bodies are enough for the God of life to work with.

If Christ's witness to God's gospel brought him into conflict with the forces that eventually crucified him, and if God's raising Christ from the dead signifies God's victory over all that would destroy abundant life, then what *theologia crucis* shows is how the core of rebellion and hope at the heart of the cross continues to sustain creative, contextually powerful theological work on behalf of those whom we continue to crucify. My hope is that, in seeing some of the ways in which this has happened in historical and contemporary theological literature, those who seek to continue to tell the truth in the face of systemic lies that kill may know that the act of such truth-telling is embedded in a powerful theological tradition that breeds both rebellion and hope, both in our own lives and in the places that our lives touch.

To join in the work of the cross is to join God's way of acting in the world, and to theologize about it is to call those within the community of fidelity to this action to be of good courage and to know that God continues to be at work in the places of pain in our world. To the extent that we too are called there, we do not go alone.

BIBLIOGRAPHY

Anselm. "Why God Became Man." In *Anselm of Canterbury: The Major Works*, edited by Brian Davies, 260–355. Oxford: Oxford University Press, 2008.

Anthony, Neal J. *Cross Narratives: Martin Luther's Christology and the Location of Redemption*. Princeton Theological Monograph Series 135. Eugene, OR: Pickwick, 2010.

Athanasius. "On the Incarnation of the Word," in *Christology of the Later Fathers,* edited by Edward Hardy, 55–110. Philadelphia: Westminster, 1954.

Bayer, Oswald. *Martin Luther's Theology: A Contemporary Interpretation*. Translated by Thomas H. Trapp. Grand Rapids: Eerdmans, 2008.

Bonhoeffer, Dietrich. *Letters and Papers from Prison (Dietrich Bonhoeffer Works, Volume 8)*. Minneapolis: Fortress, 2010.

Bouteneff, Peter, *Arvo Pärt: Out of Silence*. New York: SVS, 2015.

Brock, Rita Nakashima, and Rebecca Ann Parker. *Proverbs of Ashes: Violence, Redemptive Suffering, and the Search for What Saves Us*. Boston: Beacon, 2002.

Cherry, Kittredge, and Douglas Blanchard. *The Passion of Christ: A Gay Vision*. Berkeley, CA: Apocryphile, 2014.

Christ, P. Carol, and Judith Plaskow, eds. *WomanSpirt Rising: A Feminist Reader in Religion*. San Francisco: HarperCollins, 1992.

Cone, James. *The Cross and the Lynching Tree*. Maryknoll, NY: Orbis, 2013.

de Chergé, Christian. "The Last Testament: A Letter from the Monks of the Tibhirine." *First Things* (1996). Online: http://www.firstthings.com/article/1996/08/006-last-testament.

Ebeling, Gerhard. *Luther: An Introduction to His Thought*. Translated by R.S. Wilson. Philadelphia: Fortress, 1970.

Endo, Shusaku. *Silence.* Translated by William Johnston. Tokyo: Sophia University, 1969.

Forde, Gerhard. *On Being a Theologian of the Cross: Reflections on Luther's Heidelberg Disputation.* Grand Rapids: Eerdmans, 1997.

Francis, Leah Gunning. *Ferguson and Faith: Sparking Leadership and Awakening Community.* St. Louis, MO: Chalice, 2015.

Gavrilyuk, Paul. *The Suffering of the Impassible God: The Dialectics of Patristic Thought.* Oxford: Oxford University Press, 2004.

Gerrish, B. A. "'To the Unknown God': Luther and Calvin on the Hiddenness of God." *The Journal of Religion* 53.3 (1973) 263–92.

Gregory, Brad S. *The Unintended Reformation: How a Religious Revolution Secularized Society.* Boston, MA: Belknap, 2012.

Hall, Douglas John. *The Cross in Our Context: Jesus and the Suffering World.* Minneapolis: Fortress, 2003.

———. *Waiting for Gospel: An Appeal to the Dispirited Remnants of Protestant "Establishment."* Eugene, OR: Cascade, 2012.

Hart, David Bentley. *The Beauty of the Infinite: The Aesthetics of Christian Truth.* Grand Rapids: Eerdmans, 2004.

Iwand, Hans Joachim. "Theologia crucis." In *Nachgelassene Werke II,* edited by Helmut Gollwitzer et al., 381–398. Munich: Kaiser, 1966.

Jennings, Theodore W. *Transforming Atonement: A Political Theology of the Cross.* Minneapolis: Fortress, 2009.

Joh, Wonhee Anne. *The Heart of the Cross: A Postcolonial Christology.* Louisville: Westminster John Knox, 2006.

Jüngel, Eberhard. *God as the Mystery of the World: On the Foundation of the Theology of the Crucified One in the Dispute Between Theism and Atheism.* Translated by Darrell L. Guder. London: T. & T. Clark, 2014.

Kähler, Martin. *The So-Called Historical Jesus and the Historic Biblical Christ,* trans. Carl Braaten. Philadelphia: Fortress, 1964.

Kolb, Robert. "Luther on the Theology of the Cross," *Lutheran Quarterly* 16.4 (2002) 443–66.

Korthaus, Michael. *Kreuzestheologie: Geschichte und Gehalt eines Programmbegriffs in der evangelischen Theologie.* Tübingen: Mohr Siebeck, 2007.

Lewis, Alan. *Between Cross and Resurrection: A Theology of Holy Saturday.* Grand Rapids: Eerdmans, 2001.

Luther, Martin. *Luther's Works: Lectures on Genesis* (Volume 1). Edited by Jaroslav Pelikan. St. Louis, MO: Concordia, 1958.

———. *Luther's Works: Career of the Reformer I* (Volume 31). Edited by Harold Grimm. Philadelphia, PA: Muhlenberg, 1957.

———. *Luther's Works: Career of the Reformer IV* (Volume 34). Edited by Lewis Spitz. Philadelphia, PA: Muhlenberg, 1960.

———. *Luther's Works: Sermons I* (Volume 51). Edited and Translated by Lewis Spitz. Philadelphia, PA: Muhlenberg, 1959.

Luy, David. *Dominus Mortis: Martin Luther on the Incorruptibility of God in Christ*. Minneapolis: Fortress, 2014.

Marsh, Charles. *Strange Glory: A Life of Dietrich Bonhoeffer*. New York: Knopf, 2014.

Madsen, Anna M. *The Theology of the Cross in Historical Perspective*. Distinguished Dissertations in Christian Theology. Eugene, OR: Pickwick, 2007.

Miyamoto, Arata. *Embodied Cross: Intercontextual Reading of Theologia Crucis*. Eugene, OR: Wipf and Stock, 2010.

Moe-Lobeda, Cynthia. *Resisting Structural Evil: Love as Ecological-Economic Vocation*. Minneapolis: Fortress, 2013.

Moltmann, Jürgen. *The Crucified God: The Cross of Christ as the Foundation and Criticism of Christian Theology*. Translated by R. A. Wilson and John Bowden. Minneapolis: Fortress, 1993.

———. "The Crucified God, Yesterday and Today: 1972–2002." Translated by Margaret Kohl. In *Cross Examinations: Readings on the Meaning of the Cross Today*, edited by Marit Trelstad, 127–38. Minneapolis: Fortress, 2006.

Ngien, Dennis. *The Suffering of God According to Martin Luther's Theologia Crucis*. New York: Peter Lang, 1995.

Norris, Richard A, ed. *The Christological Controversy: Sources of Early Christian Thought*. Translated by Robert Saler. Minneapolis: Fortress, 2010.

Root, Andrew. *The Promise of Despair: The Way of the Cross as the Way of the Church*. Nashville: Abingdon, 2010.

Rossing, Barbara. *The Rapture Exposed: The Message of Hope in the Book of Revelation*. New York: Basic, 2004.

Ruge-Jones, Philip. *Cross in Tensions: Luther's Theology of the Cross as Theologico-social Critique*. Princeton Theological Monograph Series 91. Eugene, OR: Pickwick, 2008.

Rutledge, Fleming. *The Crucifixion: Understanding the Death of Jesus Christ*. Grand Rapids: Eerdmans, 2015.

Salenson, Christian. *Christian de Chergé: A Theology of Hope*. Collegeville: Liturgical, 2012.

Saler, Robert C. *Between Magisterium and Marketplace: A Constructive Account of Theology and the Church*. Minneapolis: Fortress, 2012.

———. "The Transformation of Reason in Genesis 2–3: Two Options for Theological Interpretation." *Currents in Theology and Mission* 36.4 (2009) 275–86.

Schmiechen, Peter. *Saving Power: Theories of Atonement and Forms of the Church*. Grand Rapids: Eerdmans, 2005.

Smith, James K. A. *Desiring the Kingdom: Worship, Worldview, and Cultural Formation*. Grand Rapids: Baker, 2009.

Sobrino, Jon. *The True Church and the Poor*. Eugene, OR: Wipf and Stock, 2004.

Solberg, Mary M. *Compelling Knowledge: A Feminist Proposal for an Epistemology of the Cross*. Albany: SUNY, 1997.

Song, C. S. *Jesus, the Crucified People*. Minneapolis: Fortress, 1996.

Tanner, Kathryn. *Christ the Key*. Cambridge: Cambridge University Press, 2010.

Taylor, Mark Lewis. *The Executed God: The Way of the Cross in Lockdown America*, 2nd ed. Minneapolis: Fortress, 2015.

Terrell, JoAnne Marie. "Our Mothers' Gardens: Rethinking Sacrifice." In *Cross Examinations: Readings on the Meaning of the Cross Today*, edited by Marit Trelstad, 33–49. Minneapolis: Fortress, 2006.

———. *Power in the Blood? The Cross in the African American Experience*. Eugene, OR: Wipf and Stock, 2005.

Thompson, Deanna A. "Becoming a Feminist Theologian of the Cross." In *Cross Examinations: Readings on the Meaning of the Cross Today*, edited by Marit Trelstad, 76–90. Minneapolis: Fortress, 2006.

———. *Crossing the Divide: Luther, Feminism, and the Cross*. Minneapolis: Augsburg Fortress, 2004.

Toulmin, Stephen. *Cosmopolis: The Hidden Agenda of Modernity*. Chicago: University of Chicago Press, 1990.

Treltstad, Marit, ed. *Cross Examinations: Readings on the Meaning of the Cross Today*. Minneapolis: Fortress, 2006.

Von Loewenich, Walther. *Luther's Theology of the Cross*. 5th ed. Translated by H. J. A. Bouman. Minneapolis: Augsburg, 1976.

Westhelle, Vítor. *After Heresy: Colonial Practices and Post-Colonial Theologies*. Eugene, OR: Cascade, 2010.

———. *The Church Event: Call and Challenge of a Church Protestant*. Minneapolis: Fortress, 2010.

———. "Communio Ecclesiology and the Cross: Limits and Possibilities." Online: http://download.elca.org/ELCA%20Resource%20Repository/CommunioEcclesiology.pdf.

———. *The Scandalous God: The Use and Abuse of the Cross*. Minneapolis: Fortress, 2007.

Westphal, Merold. *Suspicion and Faith: The Religious Uses of Modern Atheism*. Bronx, NY: Fordham University Press, 1998.

CPSIA information can be obtained
at www.ICGtesting.com
Printed in the USA
BVHW031938311021
620411BV00017B/191